Practicing Mindfulness: An Introduction to Meditation

Mark W. Muesse, Ph.D.

PUBLISHED BY:

THE GREAT COURSES
Corporate Headquarters
4840 Westfields Boulevard, Suite 500
Chantilly, Virginia 20151-2299
Phone: 1-800-832-2412
Fax: 703-378-3819
www.thegreatcourses.com

Mark W. Muesse, Ph.D.

W. J. Millard Professor of Religious Studies
and Director of the Asian Studies Program
Rhodes College

Professor Mark W. Muesse is the W. J. Millard Professor of Religious Studies and Director of the Asian Studies and Life: Then and Now programs at Rhodes College. He earned his bachelor of arts degree summa cum laude in English from Baylor University and a master of theological studies, a master of arts, and a doctor of philosophy in The Study of Religion from Harvard University. He has traveled extensively throughout Asia and has studied at the International Buddhist Meditation Centre in Wat Mahathat, Bangkok, Thailand; the Himalayan Yogic Institute in Kathmandu, Nepal; the Subodhi Institute in Piliyandala, Sri Lanka; and the Middle East Technical University in Ankara, Turkey.

Professor Muesse has taught at Harvard College, Harvard Divinity School, and the University of Southern Maine, where he also served as Associate Dean of the College of Arts and Sciences. In 1988, he became Assistant Professor of Religious Studies at Rhodes College. In 1995, he became Associate Professor, and he served as Chair of the Department of Religious Studies from 2004 to 2008. He teaches courses in world religion and philosophy, modern theology, and spirituality. Professor Muesse has also been Visiting Professor of Theology at the Tamilnadu Theological Seminary in Madurai, India.

Professor Muesse has produced three of The Great Courses: *Great World Religions: Hinduism*; *Religions of the Axial Age: An Approach to the World's Religions*; and *Confucius, Buddha, Jesus, and Muhammad*. He is the author of many articles and reviews on comparative religion and theology. His most recent book is *The Hindu Traditions: A Concise Introduction*.

In 2007, Professor Muesse received Fortress Press's Undergraduate Teaching Award at the American Academy of Religion's annual meeting.

In 2008, he received the Clarence Day Award for Outstanding Teaching, Rhodes College's highest honor for a member of its faculty. Known for his experiential teaching style, Professor Muesse was honored for his "effective use of imaginative and creative pedagogy" as well as his ability to motivate his students toward lifelong study.

Professor Muesse's wife, Dhammika, is a native of Sri Lanka and teaches in the Rhodes College Chemistry Department. They have a daughter, Ariyana, who attends St. Mary's Episcopal School. ∎

Table of Contents

Table of Contents

Table of Contents

SUPPLEMENTAL MATERIAL

Practicing Mindfulness: An Introduction to Meditation

Scope:

Mindfulness is the skill of being deliberately attentive to one's experience as it unfolds—without the superimposition of our usual commentary and conceptualizing. The capacity to be mindful provides a wholesome way to attend to our experiences and helps us overcome the unskillful habits of mind that cause us to suffer needlessly. This course is a practical guide to developing the skill of mindfulness and applying it to every aspect of daily life.

The foundational technique for cultivating mindfulness is the practice of meditation. Meditation is a form of physical and mental exercise that serves to strengthen the natural ability to bring moment-by-moment awareness to our lives. Since mindfulness is the skill of opening ourselves to reality without judgment, it is important that we approach the practice of meditation in this spirit, relinquishing preconceptions and expectations about the discipline. It is also essential to provide a spiritual and physical context conducive to meditation. Using the Five Precepts of Buddhism, we will consider the interconnections of ethical behavior with the development of mindfulness and the shaping of personal character. Then, we'll study the most effective postures for sitting meditation. Beginning the actual practice of meditation starts with focusing attention on the breath and observing when the mind strays. By noticing when attention has wandered away from its focal point and then gently returning it to the breath, we gradually strengthen our capacities for concentration and awareness.

Practicing mindfulness over time reveals and develops the qualities of wisdom and compassion, the twin virtues of the discipline. Wisdom means seeing clearly into the fundamental nature of reality. Through meditative practice, we can deeply recognize the eternal arising and passing away of all phenomena and see the unsatisfactory quality of ordinary human experience that derives from the illusion of the self as an entity separate from the rest of reality.

Practice is the key to mindfulness. Mindfulness techniques are skills that anyone can develop and apply to the simplest aspects of living: breathing, sensing, feeling, eating, walking, speaking, and even driving. When we've covered the fundamental aspects of mindfulness practice, we'll work on more challenging things: cultivating compassion for ourselves and others; developing a life of generosity; accepting our mortality; and coping with physical pain, grief, and anger. We'll explore difficulties often encountered in meditation and ways of working with these impediments to strengthen concentration and to counter frustration and discouragement.

Compassion—the desire to alleviate suffering—is an essential component of our nature as human beings. Mindfulness practices such as metta meditation allow us to cultivate compassion and develop empathy for others, deeply recognizing their inner experience. *Dana* (sharing with others) reveals the life-giving effects of generosity on both the giver and the receiver and helps us understand our attachment to "things." We'll also consider the ways in which both inner experience and outward action are influenced by our use of language, reflecting on four Buddhist principles of skillful communication.

Finding compassion for ourselves is more challenging for many of us, particularly the perfectionists among us; mindfulness techniques can help us embrace and accept both imperfection and perfectionism as an opening to freedom and deeper humanity. The skills of mindfulness also offer powerful means to work with physical discomfort—through understanding the crucial distinction between pain and suffering—as it directly affects our perceptions.

Reflecting on the universality of loss, we'll take a deeper look at the notion of impermanence. By learning to embrace life's transience and to center our focus in the present moment, we are able to experience loss and even grief without fear or aversion. In the mindfulness tradition, the practice of reflecting on death is considered to be both liberating and essential to living a full and satisfying life. We'll examine the ways in which our culture conditions us to avoid and deny death, and we'll learn meditations that deepen both the awareness of life's transience and our ability to live freely.

Finally, we'll reflect on the capacity of mindfulness practice to profoundly alter our perceptions of ourselves, the world, and our place in it. ■

Mindlessness—The Default Setting
Lecture 1

This course is predicated on the conviction that it is not necessary to live at the mercy of an untamed mind. By coming to understand the way our minds work, we can learn to shape our mental functions in ways that will remove the frantic, driven, distracted, semiconscious qualities from our lives. We'll learn to use mindfulness meditations and exercises to enhance our awareness of everyday experiences—such as breathing, eating, and walking—and to help us cope with the more challenging aspects of life—such as pain, grief, and anger.

Mindlessness as a Mental Condition

- Most of the time, our minds function by generating a constant swirl of remarks and judgments that create a barrier of words and images that separate us from our own lives. This mental condition of **mindlessness** makes it difficult to be mindful, or attentive, to the experiences of our lives.

- The very dynamics that lead to mindlessness can be gently redirected through meditation to cultivate the quality of mindfulness and to develop the mind in ways that will be conducive to our happiness and to the happiness of others.

- The mind is a notoriously elusive concept. We all have an intuitive idea of what we mean by it, but trying to define it concretely seems almost impossible.

- Throughout the centuries, theologians, philosophers, psychologists, and other thinkers have offered various ways of conceiving of the mind and trying to bring some specificity to the notion.

- The mind has been associated with such functions as consciousness, thought, perception, memory, emotion, willing, reasoning, and imagination—and with various combinations thereof. In this course, the mind will refer to all of these mental processes.

- In short, we'll remain content with a rather vague conception of the mind. As we proceed, we'll begin to see the value of allowing this concept to remain broad and inclusive.

Owners of Our Minds

- We ordinarily think of our minds as our own—as something belonging to ourselves and to no one else. No one can "read" our minds, but they may infer our mental states by becoming familiar with facial expressions or other gestures that coordinate with particular forms of our subjectivity.

- Scientists may be able to analyze certain brain activity using sophisticated imaging techniques, but they cannot perceive what our minds are thinking.

- We basically think of ourselves as in control of our own thought processes. Our minds are in fact our most private domains. Most people will more readily regard their minds as the locus of their true or real selves—rather than, say, their bodies.

- We usually experience our minds as somehow connected to our bodies. Specifically, the mind seems to work within the same space occupied by the head, suggesting a close relationship between mind and brain. However, specifying the exact nature of the relationship between mind and body has bedeviled thinkers for millennia.

- Despite the obvious importance that we accord the mind and the intimacy it has with our physical natures, we do not really understand it or use it very well. We pay some attention to the content of our mind, but we have little awareness of how our mind functions.

- Most of us simply have not taken the time to observe the operation of our mind. In general, we pay about as much attention to our minds as we do to the rest of our lives, which is to say, of course, not very much.

Attending to the Present

- Most of our daily lives are essentially governed by routine. The great value of these habits is that they free our minds to do other things; we do these things without having to expend precious energy trying to make up our minds.

- Unfortunately, the freedom such routines afford the mind is not well used. If they find a moment when complete attentiveness to the present is not demanded, our minds tend to gravitate to one of two places: the past or the future.

- Your thoughts may even alternate between past and future, but they will tend to avoid the present as much as possible. If you pay attention to your ordinary thought processes, you will discover that you probably spend very little time living in the present.

- Even when we find ourselves attending to the present, we may discover that what our minds churn out is fairly worthless. Most of us are constantly making instantaneous judgments about what we experience. If you allow these trains of thought to continue, you may find them leading to other thoughts and judgments that do not have any real substance.

Controlling the Mind

- We're not ordinarily in control of our minds, despite what we may think. We can't turn them off, and we can't always make them do what we want. Judgments, thoughts, and emotions seem to arise unbidden and often unwelcome.

- Rather than being in control of our minds, our minds seem to control us—compelling us, driving us, urging us in the directions it deems fit.

- Mindlessness comes at a very high cost: Living with a mind that we don't know very well, that is often out of control and semiconscious much of the time, causes us and others to suffer greatly—probably far more than we realize.

- The Buddha, an individual who knew the mind far better than most of us, put it this way: "Whatever an enemy might do to an enemy, or a foe to a foe, the ill-directed mind can do to you even worse."

- Is it any wonder we so frequently attempt to silence or alter our minds with drugs, amusements, and other forms of distraction? Fortunately, most of us don't reach a mind-driven point of despair, but we nonetheless endure the consequences of an immensely powerful but unruly mind.

Mindfulness is the power of heightened awareness and sensitivity to ourselves and our world.

- We find ourselves entertaining thoughts that serve no wholesome value in our lives. We make snap judgments about individuals based on the slimmest and most trivial of evidence. We spin out falsehoods that we ourselves come to believe. We're constantly comparing ourselves to others, a practice that inevitably leads to pain. All of this, and more, drives us to lead frenzied lives—often on the verge of misery.

- This sense of dissatisfaction, of which we are more or less conscious at different times in our lives, impels us to find something—anything—to bring relief. Unfortunately, our minds have been conditioned to seek solutions to its torment in the most unhelpful ways.

- The beliefs that compel us to keep looking somewhere else for something to bring us relief are so common that we rarely consider that it might be time to try another approach. Rather than seek happiness through the usual ineffective and often counterproductive means, this course will offer you a different way.

- It's possible to cultivate a wholesome mind that will produce thoughts that contribute to our well-being and to the well-being of the whole world. We can shape our mental functions in ways that will remove the frantic, driven, distracted, semiconscious qualities from our lives—but it will not be easy.

Conditioning the Mind

- Our minds are malleable realities; they are plastic and can be reshaped in ways that we choose. The mind, in other words, is a conditioned phenomenon.

- Perhaps we are born with certain dispositions to act and think in particular ways. Many Hindus, Buddhists, and Jains think that **karma**—our thoughts, deeds, and words from previous lives—profoundly influences the mental states we have at birth.

- Essentially, the idea of karma suggests that the way we are now is the consequence of the ways we have thought and acted up to this point. In short, we have been conditioned by ourselves and by others—whether we believe the conditioning process began in former lifetimes or whether it simply began in this lifetime.

- The term **conditioning** is a very useful one for describing this process. Habitual thinking significantly determines what we think, feel, and perceive. The more we entertain a particular thought or a particular kind of thought, the more our minds are prone to generate thoughts of that nature.

- The process of mental conditioning is so powerful that it may seem at times that our whole cerebral function is entirely determined by the factors of our biological makeup or our upbringing. However, we have a small but extremely important capacity to redirect our mind in ways that allow us to recondition it.

- In traditional philosophical terms, we are largely determined but we have a modicum of free will. In this sense, free will is not just a feature of our makeup; instead, it is something that must be exercised and developed. Without cultivation, we are vulnerable to losing the ability to act and think freely altogether.

The Mind as an Instrument

- This course will be unlike most other courses you've ever taken, in which your mind is deliberately stimulated. Stimulating the mind is valuable for many things, but it is not what this course is about. This course is for people whose minds are overstimulated and need a respite from too much thinking.

- In this course, you'll learn to think of the mind not as the center of your personality but as an instrument or tool that you can use for your happiness. Like any instrument, it's essential to learn how to use it properly and to practice using it until the skill becomes second nature.

- Throughout this course, there will be sitting meditations, guided meditations, and other exercises to do. You will need to carve out a time and place to practice them.

- Whether or not this course makes you happy or improves the quality of your life is entirely up to you. Throughout the ages, individuals who have seriously employed the methods we'll discuss have claimed to have discovered something deep and enriching by using them.

- The Buddha, who warned of the tremendously harmful potential of the undisciplined mind, also proclaimed the tremendous benefits of a well-trained mind: "Whatever a mother, father or other relative might do for you, the well-directed mind can do for you even better."

Important Terms

conditioning: The process of habitual thinking that significantly determines what people think, feel, and perceive. The more people entertain a particular thought or a particular kind of thought, the more their minds are prone to generate thoughts of that nature.

karma: The belief of many Hindus, Buddhists, and Jains that thoughts, deeds, and words from people's previous lives profoundly influence the mental states they have at birth.

mindlessness: A mental state in which the mind generates a constant swirl of remarks and judgments that create a barrier of words and images that separate people from their lives. This condition makes it difficult to be mindful—or attentive—to life's experiences.

Questions to Consider

1. How would you characterize your relationship to your mind? Is the mind something you possess, something you are, or something else?

2. Throughout your day, pay attention to your internal dialogue. Ask yourself as many times as you can remember, "What am I thinking?" Are there patterns of thought that correlate to the state of mindlessness?

Mindfulness—The Power of Awareness
Lecture 2

Mindfulness can be defined in a variety of ways, but virtually all definitions understand it as a particular kind of awareness. At its most basic level, mindfulness is a deliberate way of paying attention to what is occurring within oneself as it is happening. Mindfulness is more than just awareness, however; it is paying attention without judgment or evaluation. In recent years, mindfulness has become an especially prominent concept in contemporary psychology and medicine, where it is frequently used in connection with stress reduction and wellness.

Mindfulness and Awareness

- Most of the time, most of us exist in mindlessness, a state of semiawareness governed by habit and inattention. Mindlessness causes us to suffer—probably more than we're even aware. This ordinary mental condition is not inevitable; there is a cure for it, and it's called mindfulness, a skill that anyone can learn.

- **Mindfulness** is moment-by-moment awareness; it is the process of attentively observing your experience as it unfolds. Mindfulness allows us to become keen observers of ourselves and gradually transform the way our minds operate. With sustained practice, mindfulness can make us more attentive to our experience and less captive to the whims that drive our minds around.

- The process of mindfulness is devoid of the constant comparing and assessing that ordinarily occupies our mental functioning. When we're being mindful, we are simply being mentally alert without the overlay of our usual commentary and conceptualizing.

- Because we're not judging our experiences as right or wrong or good or bad, mindfulness is also characterized by a high degree of openness, receptivity, and inquisitiveness. With this open and attentive attitude, we're able to perceive ourselves more clearly, observing the dynamics and details that often escape our notice.

- Mindfulness is not about removing thoughts from our minds—even judgmental thoughts. It is about knowing when we're thinking and recognizing thoughts as momentary events that float through our minds.

- Because mindfulness is based on the universal human faculty of awareness, we've all had experiences very close to mindfulness. Try to recall some time in your in life when you felt especially attentive, perhaps so rapt that your usual internal dialogue was suspended as you became fully present to your experience.

- For example, people often report a heightened sense of awareness whenever their lives are endangered. The perception of slowed time in these instances is related to the sharpening of one's conscious activity as the mind marshals its resources to prevent itself from perishing. The lucid memories of these occasions are based on the same heightened awareness that characterizes mindfulness.

- When we practice mindfulness, we are doing so deliberately. We are taking the same mental functioning found within extraordinary experiences and purposefully developing and applying it to our ordinary lives. In short, we are taking a natural capacity that we usually use only on special occasions and extending its usage to every aspect of our existence.

Mindfulness and Religion

- Because it is innate to human beings, the power of mindfulness has been available to us for tens of thousands of years—but the concept of mindfulness is more recent. The historical evidence suggests that mindfulness was first widely taught 2,500 years ago by the individual known today as the Buddha.

- In his teachings, the Buddha spoke extensively of *sati*, a special form of heightened awareness that promoted the end of suffering and fostered happiness and well-being for all. *Sati* is the Buddha's word that we now translate into English as "mindfulness." According to the Buddha's teachings, mindfulness is essential to eliminating delusion and seeing the world and ourselves as they truly are.

- Although Buddhism has devoted more energy to the study and practice of mindfulness than any other religion, every major religious tradition prescribes something akin to it. These practices are not always as prominent in other religions as they are in Buddhism, but they can often be found within a religion's contemplative and esoteric dimensions.

- Mindfulness is not a discipline that is limited to religion. Forms of mindfulness practice can be found in many schools of secular philosophy in both the East and West.

Historical evidence suggests that mindfulness was first widely taught 2,500 years ago by the Buddha.

- In Buddhism, mindfulness is a component of the **Eightfold Path** that leads to enlightenment and freedom from the cycle of continual rebirth. Mindfulness thus serves the purpose of advancing one's quest for **nirvana**.

- In the Christian traditions, mindfulness is often understood to bring one closer to God and to a life of greater holiness, but it has never been regarded as essential to salvation because Christianity grounds redemption on belief and doctrine.

- In Hinduism, mindfulness is said to peel away the many layers of illusion that veil our clear perception of the ultimate reality.

- In Confucianism, mindfulness is part of moral self-cultivation, the regimen that enables individuals to realize their full humanity.

- In all traditions, mindfulness is seen a means to transform one's life in meaningful and wholesome ways.

Benefits of Mindfulness

- One does not need to regard mindfulness in metaphysical categories to find it an extremely beneficial practice. Without discounting the religious and theological interpretations, it is possible to spell out the very pragmatic value of mindfulness for living a more vital and happier life.

- The chief goal of mindfulness, as its definition implies, is increased awareness. Its other benefits, while considerable and of immense value, are essentially of secondary importance. In other words, everything else you might gain from a mindfulness practice depends on strengthening your faculty of awareness.

- Although it is used for these purposes, mindfulness is not fundamentally about relaxation, stress reduction, or even self-improvement. It is about knowing yourself and your world better and more clearly—the kind of knowing that comes only with experience, with seeing things for yourself.

- With mindfulness, you can see how your mind operates and responds to its world. Because mindfulness requires us to focus attention on what is happening within ourselves and our environment as it is occurring, you can be consciously present for your life.

- We learn in the mindfulness disciplines that there is a lot in the world over which we have no control. Mindfulness teaches this fact not as an abstract idea to which we give assent, but as a concrete and clearly demonstrated reality. At the same time, mindfulness teaches that one of the things that we can change is the operation of our own minds.

- Ordinarily, our responses to the elements of life that are out of our control are determined by our conditioning. We tend to act out of habit—without much thought—unaware that we can be more deliberate about the way we allow events beyond our power to affect us.

- Practicing mindfulness can give us a mental spaciousness that offers us greater freedom to shape the kind of person we will become. Mental spaciousness is of immense value in helping us manage the seemingly incessant colloquy of judgments and commentary that constitutes the mindless state. It allows us to recognize the patterns of thinking that are detrimental to the well-being of ourselves and others and enables us to relinquish them and render them harmless.

- Likewise, mindfulness helps us work with difficult emotional states such as anger, greed, and fear, providing us with the resources to act on these states in ways that are beneficial rather than damaging. With dedicated practice you can really learn to handle your anger effectively, to want less, and to be courageous and compassionate.

Mindfulness and Health

- Mindfulness is not only about the mind; it is an invaluable tool in helping us cope with our bodies. Medical science in the last quarter century has amassed an impressive collection of evidence that conclusively demonstrates that mindfulness practice has a salutary effect on health.

- One study recently presented to the American Heart Association showed that patients who practiced mindfulness regularly reduced by half their risk of heart attacks, strokes, and death from all causes as compared with similar patients who were only given education about healthy living and diet.

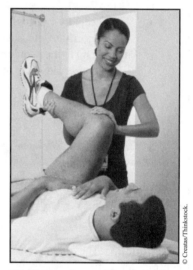

© Creatas/Thinkstock.

- In addition, a recent meta-analysis—a study of the scientific quality of these studies of mindfulness—concluded that the proposition that mindfulness practices are beneficial to health is a legitimate and empirically verifiable claim.

- Although it is clear that mindfulness offers valuable and even amazing contributions to our physical and psychological well-being,

Mindfulness is used in connection with stress reduction and wellness in contemporary medicine.

it is still unable to stave off the inevitable demise of our bodies. No matter how healthy we have been, each of us will die, and the practice of mindfulness cannot change that reality.

- Mindfulness can help us accept the reality of death and prepare us for the moment when we draw our last breath. One of the essential lessons these practices reveal to us is that life is ephemeral, and denying that only causes great suffering and unhappiness. Genuinely accepting the impermanence of life, however, is liberating and allows us to be happy.

- Just as we learn to accept the loss of our bodies to death, mindfulness practice helps us to accept the loss of everything. Life is such that every one of us must bear a tremendous measure of grief. Mindfulness teaches us to prepare for the inevitability of death and to accept it—not with stoic resignation, but with joy and contentment.

- The acceptance of loss actually helps us relax and be less anxious. The majority of our actions suggest that we believe acquiring and holding on to the people and things that give us pleasure will put our lives at ease. However, it is only by relinquishing our attachment to everything we think will make us happy that we can actually be happy. Mindfulness allows us to see this truth and empowers us to act on it.

Important Terms

Eightfold Path: In Buddhism, mindfulness is a component of this path, which leads to enlightenment and freedom from the cycle of continual rebirth.

mindfulness: The process of attentively observing an experience as it unfolds in a moment-by-moment awareness; it is devoid of the constant comparing and assessing that ordinarily occupies our mental functioning.

nirvana: A state of bliss; in Buddhism, it transcends suffering and karma.

sati: A special form of heightened awareness that promotes the end of suffering and fosters happiness and well-being for all; it is the Buddha's word that is translated into English as "mindfulness."

Questions to Consider

1. Can you recall moments in which you have become fully aware of your ordinary experience without the imposition of judgments or other thoughts?

2. Try to notice the times when you suddenly become aware of what is going on around you. It may feel as if you have been pulled out of a dream into a wakening moment.

3. How could mindfulness training help you as an individual? How would you expect mindfulness to help you the most in your life?

Expectations—Relinquishing Preconceptions
Lecture 3

Mindfulness is a function of our mental faculties that we all use to a small degree in our everyday life. Our objective in this course is to understand that function better and learn to develop it so that we are able to use it to a greater extent throughout every aspect of our existence. For millennia, individuals throughout the world have been studying mindfulness and cultivating ways to refine its usage, and we'll be relying on their wisdom to guide us.

Mindfulness and Meditation

- The principal instrument for strengthening our capacity for mindfulness is a practice widely known as meditation. Mindfulness and meditation are not synonymous terms, but they appear together so frequently in print and in discourse that one might easily think they were.

- Mindfulness refers to the power of our minds to give close, nonjudgmental attention to our experience as it unfolds. **Meditation** refers to certain exercises that can be used to enlarge and refine mindfulness. Not all forms of meditation, however, intend to cultivate mindfulness.

- Some meditative practices are oriented toward generating transcendent experiences, achieving a trance state, or gaining extraordinary powers, but the particular types of meditation we'll discuss in this course are practices whose central purpose is to make us more mindful.

- Meditation helps us become more mindful by providing us with specific ways to train our awareness. In this sense, meditation gives us a particular context in which to work at putting our minds in better condition.

- Some of the ideas people have about meditation may fit other forms of the disciplines that go by that name, but they may not be correct for mindfulness meditation. Therefore, whatever preconceived ideas you may have about this practice, begin to relinquish them—another exercise in mindfulness.

Preconceptions about Meditation

It's Not Just Thinking

- Meditation usually suggests a form of deep thinking, the kind of mental activity associated with taking a thought or a problem and intensely reflecting on it—mulling it over in the mind.

- This kind of deliberate thought process is a very important mental activity, but it is not the kind of discipline that helps develop mindfulness. In fact, it is quite possible to ruminate or think over an idea without being mindful. Awareness and thinking are two different mental functions.

- Interestingly, the tradition on which mindfulness practice is founded does not use the term

Practices like meditation and yoga are rapidly becoming a part of our cultural mainstream.

meditation. Buddhism calls this practice ***bhavana***, which is most accurately translated as "cultivation." *Bhavana* does not mean deep thinking but, rather, the awareness and discipline that allow one to shape the mind in ways conducive to happiness and well-being.

- When the Buddha chose this word for the practices that enhance mindfulness, he was selecting an ordinary agricultural metaphor, an image deeply resonant with the common people of his day. He was comparing the process of developing the mind to the way that farmers prepare and care for the land to produce a rich, nourishing crop.

It's Not Exotic

- Meditation is not exotic, at least not in the way that we will study and practice it. Given its early associations with Hindu gurus and Buddhist monks, many in the Western world have come to regard meditation practice as rather strange and foreign.

- For some, the aura of exoticism exerts a compelling attraction. They become interested in meditation precisely because it smacks of the unusual, the mystical, and the esoteric.

- Others, however, might find the aura of exoticism repellant. We have an ingrained tendency to view different practices and beliefs with suspicion, if not outright fear.

- The "other"—as philosophers call people and things different from us—often threatens our sense of identity and security; hence, we tend to discount or disparage the other. Although meditation and yoga are rapidly becoming a part of our cultural mainstream, for many, meditation still retains a sense of otherness.

- Those who are attracted to meditation and those who are repulsed by it because of its exotic quality are both mistaken. Meditation, at least mindfulness meditation, is profoundly ordinary; there is really nothing extraordinary or strange about it.

- If you take up meditation because you think it is exotic or because you want to be pious and deepen your spirituality, your attraction to meditation may simply arise from the ego—the desire to appear other than you actually are.

- It is perfectly fine to begin a mindfulness practice because it seems exotic or because it serves your ego needs in some way. Ultimately, it does not matter why you start, but for mindfulness practice to become truly constructive in your life, your initial motives will have to be relinquished.

It's Not an Extraordinary Experience

- Like the attraction to its exotic trappings, some people take up meditation because they seek certain extraordinary experiences or altered states of consciousness. Again, such motivations are fine at the start, but for mindfulness meditation, they will need to be eventually given up.

- Mindfulness is not about having unusual or transcendent experiences. Strange, fascinating, and mysterious experiences may, in fact, occur while you are meditating; with meditation, it is possible to have any kind of experience imaginable.

- Particular kinds of experiences are not the goal of meditating. Rather, we are seeking to develop a way to relate to all of our experiences, regardless of their quality or content.

It's Not Easy or Fast

- Today especially, many people become interested in meditation because they are attracted to the possibility of reducing the stress in their lives and becoming a more relaxed person. Like beginning meditation to serve one's ego needs, starting a practice to relax and become calmer is perfectly fine.

- Although greater serenity is indeed one of the results of meditation, tranquility is often not realized early in the practice. Consequently, many people have disappointing experiences with their first encounters with meditation. For the vast majority of practitioners, meditation is not easy and its benefits are not quickly realized.

- It makes sense that many people show up to learn meditation thinking that it will be a swift solution to their problems. We live in an impatient culture that has come to expect quick fixes. Mindfulness meditation can teach us to be more patient, but we have to be patient to learn that lesson.

- Particularly in the beginning stages, meditating can also be very difficult. Most of us are not accustomed to sitting still for very long. In addition, being alone with your thoughts can be terrifying, which is why many people avoid it at all costs. Stored in that awesome brain are many dreadful things, as you well know.

It's Not an Escape from Reality

- Some people consider meditation to be an escape from reality, but this is another common misconception. Given its bold intention to attend unflinchingly to all of our experiences without judgment, it is more precise to call mindfulness meditation an escape into reality.

- From the perspective of mindfulness, our lives as we ordinarily live them seem profoundly out of touch with what is real. Few people appear to live in accord with what seem to be sobering truths—that death will overtake us all, that the world is in constant change, that suffering is pervasive.

- Instead, what seem to be escapes from reality include such activities as racing about in hot pursuit of trivial successes, possessions, and pleasures; working and amusing ourselves to death; and filling our minds with useless junk.

It's Not Self-Centered

- Just as meditation has sometimes been criticized as escapist, it has also been charged with being self-centered. The expression "navel-gazing" has entered the English language as a term to refer to both meditation and egotism. In the view of some, both are forms of self-absorption.

- While the practice of mindfulness meditation no doubt begins with turning inward toward one's own experience, the sharp distinction between self and world gradually begins to fade.

- A mindfulness practice reveals the intricate ways our lives are intertwined with one another. As a consequence, meditation begins to awaken our empathy and helps develop our natural sense of compassion.

- In the Buddhist tradition, compassion and wisdom are twin virtues, and both are cultivated by the practice of meditation. It is not possible to have true wisdom without genuine compassion, and vice versa.

- To be wise is to see things clearly—without delusion. Wisdom thus means to recognize the interdependence of our life with the lives of others, and seeing our interdependence with others evokes our compassion. Therefore, a meditation practice that produces only self-satisfaction is not a genuine mindfulness practice.

© Comstock/Thinkstock.

Mindfulness practice is not as easy as it is portrayed to be on the covers of yoga magazines.

It's Not a Success-or-Failure Practice

- Conventional ideas of success and failure may also need to be abandoned when you take up meditation. In fact, you'll probably discover that you have a hard time figuring out what you need to do with your body, how to focus your attention, and what do with your mind. When you're unable to follow the instructions exactly, you may be tempted to judge your effort as a failure—but that would be a mistake.

- In meditation practice, you fail only when you do not pay attention, but even failing to pay attention is not a failure if you realize you're not paying attention. Eventually, you'll see that you cannot fail at meditation, if you just do it. By the same token, you'll see that you cannot succeed at it either.

- Meditation practice is an activity that is best approached with an openness of mind and sincerity of heart. If you can't muster openness and sincerity, that's fine—meditation can teach you that as well.

Important Terms

bhavana: Most accurately translated as "cultivation," this is what Buddhism calls meditation. It does not mean deep thinking but, rather, the awareness and discipline that allow one to shape the mind in ways conducive to happiness and well-being.

meditation: Refers to certain exercises that can be used to enlarge and refine mindfulness. Not all forms of meditation, however, intend to cultivate mindfulness.

1. What preconceptions do you bring to the practice of meditation? Why is it important to relinquish both positive and negative ideas about meditation?

2. Meditation has appeared throughout history in different forms. In your particular faith, philosophy, or practice, is meditation—or something like it—encouraged?

Preparation—Taking Moral Inventory
Lecture 4

Conduct a moral inventory in the spirit of five moral aspirations: harming others, stealing, sexual misconduct, lying, and intoxication. Consider whether any of your behaviors in these five areas might in some way impede your attentiveness to your experience and jeopardize your happiness. You'll find this exercise more meaningful if you write down your reflections. If your reflections reveal that your conduct falls short of what you think it should be, consider taking these five vows—or whichever ones you find relevant.

Mindfulness and Morality

- The religious and philosophical traditions that promote mindfulness foreground the significance of the connection between personal conduct and the practice of mindfulness in the discipline. Many of the psychological and medical approaches to mindfulness, though, tend to downplay it.

- However, to some extent, all mindfulness perspectives recognize that meditation must be practiced within the wider context of one's life, and that context necessarily involves the dimension of human experience we call ethical. The religious and philosophical traditions insist that this larger context must be in place before one attempts to delve deeper into mindfulness meditation.

- It is not possible to compartmentalize the various aspects of our lives. Our physical, mental, ethical, and spiritual dimensions are interrelated; we are holistic beings. A disordered ethical life will disrupt our efforts to practice meditation.

- The mindfulness approach to matters of personal ethics differs from moral perspectives that are governed by rules. Unlike ethical systems based on obedience to specific regulations, the practices governing ethical conduct in the mindfulness tradition are centrally concerned with shaping personal character.

- The precepts associated with mindfulness practice are put forth as tools for refining the personal qualities that enable us to become wiser and more compassionate—the principal virtues in this tradition. Observing these precepts is considered essential to sharpening the skills of mindfulness and, hence, to eliminating suffering and fostering happiness.

- The particular formulation of these principles that we'll use for this course comes from the teachings of the Buddha, but the principles are not uniquely Buddhist. In fact, most of them are included in almost all ethical perspectives—religious and secular.

- What distinguishes the Buddhist articulation is the way they are presented as aspirations rather than as commands or laws. Each of these precepts is formulated as a promise that one makes to try to behave in a specific way.

- If one falls short of the promise, he or she simply takes note of the shortcoming and vows to do better on the next occasion—without the feeling of moral guilt. Gradually, the skill to follow the precepts becomes increasingly stronger, to the point where acting otherwise becomes unthinkable.

- This particular way of approaching ethical conduct invites individuals to act morally—not to avoid punishment, but for the more positive purpose of refining one's character and promoting the well-being of the world. Attending to one's actions for this reason helps one recognize how wholesome actions condition a wholesome mind, promoting a sense of greater responsibility for the quality of our personality.

- When we fall short of our aspirations, we simply relinquish our mistake and try again. This pattern of observing and letting go is the basic dynamic of mindfulness. Thus, in attending to our conduct, we aren't only cultivating an appropriate context for mindfulness; we're actually practicing mindfulness as we do so.

The Five Ethical Aspirations

- The Buddha taught a great number of ethical aspirations to his followers, but we need only concern ourselves with five, the foundational precepts of them all. These promises are all related to the principle of not harming—a notion that resounds throughout the world's philosophical and ethical traditions.

I will endeavor not to harm sentient beings.

- From a metaphysical perspective, one might argue that harming sentient beings—beings that can feel pain and pleasure—is a violation of our innate nature or that it defies the dignity and inherent worth of others. More pragmatically, not harming others minimizes the chances that we ourselves will be harmed because people have a tendency to retaliate against those who hurt them.

- From a mindfulness perspective, striving not to cause harm helps us to be more mindful. Deliberately hurting others has a profound effect on our state of mind. Causing harm to others thus causes harm to us.

- Generally, the intention to harm arises from anger, hatred, or fear. When we act on that intention, we reinforce the emotion that underlies it, thus increasing the likelihood that the emotion will arise again.

- When our minds are flooded with anger, hatred, and fear, we lose our capacity to view things clearly, and we often make poor choices. By refusing to inflict injury when such negative emotions occur, we are given an opportunity to seek more constructive and skillful ways to respond to them.

- Not all harm we cause, however, is intentional; we often hurt others simply by being thoughtless. To vow not to harm is a promise to be more aware of our words and actions and their effect on others. It is an intention to be more mindful and to refuse to revert to the mindless state where selfishness rules.

- When we consider the unintended harm we may cause, fulfilling the first mindfulness precept seems impossible. The value of the precept, however, lies not in performing it perfectly, which we may never do, but in the objective to become more fully aware of ourselves.

I will endeavor not to steal.

- The promise not to steal follows a universal moral principle. No ethical system condones stealing, except in the rarest of cases. Proscribing stealing is an absolute necessity for the sustainability of any society.

- Whereas the intention to harm arises out of anger, hatred, and fear, stealing is usually motivated by greed and envy. Like anger, hatred, and fear, greed and envy are disruptive to the mental serenity that mindfulness needs and intends to develop.

© Photos.com/Thinkstock.

- Stealing, however, need not be prompted by greed or envy. Lurking behind so much of what we do is a self

Although some people might pilfer a few office supplies from work, most don't steal cars or televisions.

that wants godlike powers: to be at the center of the universe, to exert control over reality, to feel unconstrained by anything. The problem is that for finite beings like us, these desires are not only unrealistic—they lead to behaviors that thwart our happiness and cause misery to others.

- Stealing need not be defined merely as the taking of material things. The more insidious forms of theft are of the abstract variety, such things as taking credit for another person's ideas or illegally downloading music from the Internet. Because we live in a materialistic culture, these types of stealing often seem less real or less severe than stealing tangible objects.

- From the mindfulness perspective, there is little difference between the kinds of things one steals—the effect is the same. Taking what does not belong to us strengthens a sense of self that is unwholesome and obstructs the clarity that mindfulness practice seeks to develop.

- The promise not to steal signals our intention to restrain greed and envy and commits us to a practice of honesty, especially when we think we have the opportunity to escape without penalty. In mindfulness practice, every act leaves its mark on our character, and the small things we do, or do not do, add up.

I will endeavor not to misuse sexuality.

- Like stealing, the principle of not misusing sexuality is a near-universal ethical standard—and with good reason. The abuse of sexuality causes tremendous destruction to individual lives and threatens the stability of human social life.

- Although the proscription of abusing sexuality is a near-universal principle, the concrete meaning of that principle often varies from culture to culture. The vagueness of the mindfulness precept is deliberate and, perhaps, constructive.

- Simply vowing not to misuse sexuality, rather than promising to act on more specific rules, ultimately implies that we must take responsibility for our own sexual ethic. Because we're ultimately responsible in these situations, we must remain keenly attentive to our thoughts, words, and deeds and act in a manner that refrains from harming others and ourselves.

- The misuse of sexuality can be an especially powerful threat to mindfulness. As our own culture amply shows, sexuality can easily become an obsession that renders us mindless. Even more serious are all the things a sexually obsessed individual might be willing to do to satisfy his or her lust.

- Deeper still is the effect of a disordered sexuality on the mind. We spend so much of our lives looking for something that will make us happy—only to find that nothing provides it. The desire for happiness is wholesome, but our quest is misguided because of our distorted ideas about what will give us the satisfaction we crave.

I will endeavor not to use false speech.

- False speech is lying, gossiping and slander, cursing and harsh language, and idle chatter—frivolous talk with no constructive purpose. Try to go an entire day avoiding these forms of false speech and being attentive to the times you slip.

- The real challenge of observing this precept is to be aware of when we use false speech. We are so conditioned to this kind of behavior that we're usually oblivious when our tongues go astray until after the fact, and even then, some of us remain totally unaware of the effects of our language.

- In view of the damage caused by our mindless words and the attentiveness required to keep them in check, the significance of the promise to watch our language for mindfulness practice ought to be apparent.

I will endeavor not to consume toxins.

- Historically, the precept to refrain from consuming toxins referred specifically to the use of alcohol, but the intent of this principle was simply to diminish the destructive effects of drunkenness and to foster the clarity of mind necessary for practicing mindfulness.

- The use of alcohol can obviously affect the ability to be attentive and think clearly, but alcohol isn't the only substance that stupefies the mind. Adhering to the spirit of this precept would necessarily mean becoming aware of any substance that could impair our mental and bodily functions, such as tobacco and mind-altering drugs.

- In short, promising to observe this precept means nothing less than trying to stay as physically healthy and as mentally sharp as possible by keeping a close eye on the things we allow into our bodies and into our minds.

- Today, guarding our minds from intoxication would necessarily include being mindful about the kinds of information we take in. Surely, the amount and quality of data we permit into our heads shapes the character of our minds. And, like other stupefying substances, we can become addicted to media stimulation.

- Try to spend a day fasting from the media—that is, going 24 hours without reading a paper or magazine, listening to music, watching television, going to a movie, playing video games, or using the Internet or cell phones (except in an emergency). Those who find the fast refreshing and those who find it irritating both attest to the way heavy reliance on media stimulation can detract from mindfulness.

1. What is the relationship between moral conduct and mindfulness?

2. Dedicate a weekday to observing how well you follow each of the five precepts. For example, on Monday, watch your capacity to refrain from harming; on Tuesday, see how well you refrain from stealing, and so on.

Position—Where to Be for Meditation
Lecture 5

Establishing a suitable setting for practicing mindfulness is not complicated or difficult, but it requires some forethought and perhaps a bit of imagination and experimentation. The basic physical preparations for beginning a practice to cultivate the mind include putting the body in a safe, pleasant environment and taking up a posture that will allow it to remain still and feel stable for a longer-than-usual period. With these external factors in place, the mind will start to follow and will find it easier to become calm and focused.

Establishing a Suitable Setting

- Because our minds have been conditioned to become easily distracted, it is essential to set aside a special place and time to minimize those distractions and allow the mind to concentrate on learning to concentrate. As the mind is reconditioned in more skillful ways, it will become easier to move beyond the special practice setting to everyday life.

- This is not to say, however, that you should strictly confine your practice to special times and places until you've mastered mindfulness. Exercising mindfulness in a special context is intended only to support the development of moment-to-moment awareness throughout the rest of our lives.

Three Key Elements

Determining the Most Appropriate Time for Your Practice

- Deciding on the best time to practice meditation is probably the most individual of all the decisions you'll make concerning the external factors of this discipline. You alone are able to determine the best time to practice, and you may have to try different times to figure out your answer.

- Because you'll ultimately want to set aside about 20–45 minutes for your daily meditation, it is important to decide when you can carve out that much time to be free from interruptions or other distractions.

- You'll also want to take into consideration the times your body and mind are most conducive to practice. You might even dabble with times that seem counterintuitive.

- Less important than the time of day is the regularity with which you practice; it matters greatly that you make an effort on a daily basis. At first, it will probably be difficult to devote 20–45 minutes a day to the practice, so 5 minutes is fine as long as you commit to a regular schedule.

- As the benefits of the discipline become more apparent, you'll find it easier to make time to practice, and you'll probably begin to protect those times with great zeal. However, do not expect this at first; the benefits of mindfulness practice are gradual and cumulative.

- Finally, you should have access to a timer of some sort. The timer allows you to determine before you start how long you intend to practice, and it will help keep you committed to fulfilling that intention.

Creating the Most Congenial Location for Your Practice

- Your physical environment needs to be conducive to the facilitation of moment-to-moment awareness. Accordingly, the place you choose to meditate needs to be as quiet as possible and free from distractions and interruption.

- Whether you create a special space or just use a chair in the dining room, you may find it helpful to use the same place each time you practice. Returning to the same location helps your mind and body readily prepare for meditation and obviates the need to become familiar with a new setting.

- Ideally, your practice space should be relatively free of visual as well as other distractions—especially noise. It is very important that your practice space be pleasant; it should be inviting and calming in whatever way you see fit.

- If you're a traditionalist, you may find the time-honored forest setting to your liking. In the ancient days, when the techniques of yoga and mindfulness were being refined and practiced by great numbers of people in South Asia, it was customary to meditate out of doors.

- Most importantly, the Hindu **Upanishads**, some of the earliest documents to record instructions in contemplative practice, urge the aspirant to find a quiet, safe, uncluttered, and agreeable place to practice.

Learning to Put the Body in a Proper Position for Meditation

- Like time and place, the bodily posture for meditation practice is governed by the aim of crafting a calm and alert mind. To create these conditions, it is helpful, at least initially, to bring the body into a still and stable position.

- The classic position for meditating, of course, is sitting. Seasoned meditators, in fact, often refer to the discipline simply as "sitting" or "sitting practice." Just as one can be mindful anywhere, one can cultivate mindfulness skills in any physical position—including standing, lying down, and walking.

- With practice, the unaccustomed body can be trained to sit directly on the ground in, for example, the classic **lotus position**. In this traditional pose, one sits on the bare floor or a thin cushion and places the right foot on top of the left thigh and the left foot on top of the right thigh.

- While it is relatively easy to get into the full lotus position, maintaining it can be quite difficult and painful for the novice. Using a cushion or chair works just as well in the beginning, and the urgency of getting to mindfulness practice outweighs the need to learn the traditional position.

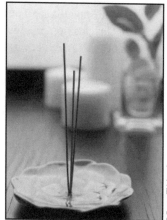

- If you choose to use a cushion, find one that will elevate your body at least five to six inches from the floor—maybe more if you are tall. This elevation allows you to cross your legs comfortably without tiring too quickly and permits necessary circulation throughout the body.

Your meditation practice space should be pleasant; some people prefer to scent it with incense.

- You will also find it very helpful to wear loose-fitting, comfortable clothes for your practice. In addition, you should remove your shoes because shoes can restrict the flow of circulation—just as tight-fitting clothes can.

- What is wonderful about sitting on a cushion is that you don't have to entangle your legs in the compact way required by the lotus position. You may simply cross your legs at the ankles without having to place your feet on opposite thighs—a position known as the **Burmese style**.

- A posture called *seiza* involves sitting on your calves with your knees, shins, and feet resting on the ground. This manner of sitting is very common throughout Japan, even among those who do not practice meditation.

- Using a chair for mindfulness practice is almost the same as using it for ordinary sitting—but with a few important exceptions. First, you should keep both feet flat on the floor without crossing them. This position promotes a feeling of stability and prevents cramping or other painful sensations.

- Second, you should not use the back of the chair for support. Sit away from the back of the chair to avoid leaning on it. Although it feels more comfortable initially, you will soon be tired and will find yourself moving your body to find a more comfortable position. Remember, we are seeking a posture that will enable us to avoid unnecessary movement.

- All forms of sitting—on the ground, on a cushion, on a bench, and in a chair—are designed to prevent the back from resting against an external object. The purpose of this design is to encourage the back to remain in a position conducive to mental alertness and the smooth flow of breathing.

The Position of the Back

- Wherever you choose to sit, the position of the back will be ultimately the same. Keep your back straight but not rigid. There should be a slight curvature following the natural contours of the spine. To achieve this

The place you choose to meditate needs to be quiet and free from distractions and interruptions.

© Valueline/Thinkstock.

position, you may find it helpful to roll your hips forward a bit as you elongate your back.

- Regardless of what you sit on, it may be useful to imagine a string attached to the crown of your skull that is pulling it upward toward the ceiling. This visualization helps lengthen the backbone while drawing down the shoulders and keeping the head in its proper position for practice.

- At first, remaining in this position may be uncomfortable because we are not accustomed to using the lower back muscles in this way. Over time, though, those muscles will strengthen and maintaining this posture will not be difficult at all.

- Now that you have found a steady place for your legs, focus your attention on the back. Allow it to elongate and follow its natural curvature. Permit your shoulders to relax by coaxing them down toward the floor and drawing them toward the spine.

Other Physical Preparations

- With legs and back in place, we can now attend to the hands and arms. Traditionally, the upper extremities find their place in two locations. First, you may put the hands in your lap, one on top of the other. A second approach is to place the hands on the knees—either palms down or up.

- You will probably need to experiment with your arms and hands to decide which position is right for you. Your criteria for making this determination are comfort and stability: Choose the posture that allows you to remain still for the longest period.

- With the chin essentially level with the floor, we now consider what to do with the various elements of the head. Because a great deal of muscular tension accrues in this region of the body, try to relax those muscles systematically. Move your jaw around and allow it to hang slightly from the rest of the head. Keep your lips lightly closed or slightly parted. Let your tongue relax in your mouth.

- Next, you must decide what to do with your eyes. You can meditate with the eyes open or shut; both approaches have their advantages. Keeping the eyes closed helps eliminate external visual distractions, but closed eyes permit a range of rather amazing internal distractions.

- Open-eye practice, though, promotes alertness. You may find that keeping your eyes closed for an extended time makes you drowsy, but keeping the eyes open works against that. If you choose to practice with open eyes, you should direct your vision to a point on the ground in front of you about six feet away from your body.

- You may wish to try both open and closed eyes to determine which approach is most helpful. If you have never practiced meditative disciplines before, you might want to begin with closed eyes simply to assist in removing visual distraction and promoting concentration. Later, you can try to practice with eyes open and see how that style suits you.

Important Terms

Burmese style: In this position, one sits on a cushion, crossing the legs at the ankles without having to place the feet on opposite thighs—as when sitting on the floor.

lotus position: In this traditional pose, one sits on the bare floor or a thin cushion and places the right foot on top of the left thigh and the left foot on top of the right thigh.

seiza: A posture that involves sitting on one's calves with the knees, shins, and feet resting on the ground. This manner of sitting is very common throughout Japan, even among those who do not practice meditation.

Upanishad: One of the earliest Hindu documents in which instructions in contemplative practice were recorded.

1. Why is it important to set aside a specific place and time for practicing mindfulness?

2. If you have chosen a time and place for your sitting practice, how does the environment make you feel? Relaxed, anxious, happy, or uncomfortable? Is there anything you can do to make the setting more conducive to meditating?

Breathing—Finding a Focus for Attention
Lecture 6

You can imagine the mind in its usual state as a bottle of muddy water. Your thoughts are swirling and chaotic; it's not easy to think clearly in this situation. However, if you simply set the jar down and refrain from stirring it up, the dirt will settle and the water will become clear as the sediment simply falls to the bottom. When the mind is given a chance, it will naturally settle and become clear and serene—just like muddy water.

Preparing the Mind and Body

- To allow our mind to settle, we need a focus, or an anchor—a fixed place to direct our attention while the mind calms itself. This anchor serves the same purpose as setting down a jar of muddy water. It simply helps keep us from stirring things up.

- As we continue with instructions for beginning to meditate, try to read while sitting in one of the meditative postures described earlier. This will help condition your body to the proper position, and you'll be prepared to follow instructions as they are presented. When your body is properly positioned, take a few deep breaths to help you settle in.

- As your sitting meditation proceeds, you may discover that some part of your body requires readjustment. If you find yourself needing to shift your body a bit, it is perfectly fine to do so. You goal is not to remain absolutely still but to attain some reasonable stability that allows you to focus on developing your awareness.

- As you meditate, it's a good idea to occasionally check each of the items mentioned for posture to ensure that your body is in the best position possible. The only rule is that if you make adjustments during your practice, do so with complete mindfulness.

Attending to the Mind

- Once the body is where it needs to be, we turn our attention to the mind. We take a brief moment to acknowledge our intention to practice mindfulness. As we deepen our practice, we will discover how critical it is to set proper intentions; when we are sincere and determined about our purposes, they have an amazing capacity to be realized.

- Now, we are ready to begin the meditation. Our initial task is to establish a focal point, or anchor. What we wish to do is to let the mind settle down, like a jar of muddy water, allowing its mindless hyperactivity to subside gradually.

- All forms of meditation use such an anchor, although the particular focal point varies from tradition to tradition. Some practitioners use a **mantra**, which is usually a short saying or set of syllables that the meditator repeats to him- or herself. Virtually anything—an object, a sound, a thought, or a bodily sensation—can become the focus of meditative practice.

Attending to the Breath

- In the basic mindfulness exercises taught here, we use the breath as the anchor for our attention. Although we will not focus solely on the breath, at the beginning of our training, it is a good place to start.

- For one thing, the breath is always present. Because of this, the breath is something to which we can return—no matter where we are—when our mind begins to wander, as it inevitably will. That fact is essential to strengthening our powers of concentration.

- Second, simply attending to the rhythms of breathing as we inhale and exhale brings profound calmness to the body. Watching the breath serves two important purposes: to calm us and to focus our awareness. Observing the breath can also teach us many things about the world and about ourselves, as we will see when we start to meditate.

- There are several ways you can observe the breath, and you'll need to experiment a bit to see which technique works best for you. First, you can watch your breath by focusing attention on the sensations of the air flowing through your nostrils. Simply pay attention to where the sensation feels most prominent and direct your awareness to that area. Take a few moments to try this technique.

- A second way to observe breathing is by attending to the abdomen or the chest as either expands and contracts with each breath. You may prefer directing your concentration to one of these locations if the sensation at the nostrils seems too subtle or too faint to hold your attention. Again, take a moment to try this method. Simply guide your awareness to the place where you most prominently sense the rhythms of your inhalation and exhalation.

- As you advance in your practice, you may discover other places to attend to your breathing, which is fine. The important thing is to choose a site and stay with it, at least in the initial training stages. The breath functions as a focal point for awareness, so that point needs to remain constant.

- Once you have determined where you will observe your breath, then sit there and watch yourself breathe. Now, stay there for a few moments and pay attention to your breath. Let your breathing be as effortless as possible. Just let it be what it will be.

- Your task is merely to watch what happens. If you can do this, you are being mindful. Pay attention to the minute qualities of this process, but refrain from making judgments or evaluating your experience.

- Try to notice the things you usually ignore. Observe the start of your inhalation; observe when the inhaled breath has come to an end. Then, watch as you begin to exhale, and watch as the exhalation comes to an end. As you focus on your breathing, try to remain merely observant, and stay attentive to your breath for as long as you can.

Breathing and Mindfulness

- No matter how hard we try, it's very difficult at the beginning of this discipline to stay concentrated. After only a short time, attention usually begins to wander elsewhere, and a torrent of thoughts and judgments flood the brain.

- When you notice that your mind has wandered away from its focal point, simply observe the fact that it has strayed and then—ever-so gently—return your attention to the breath. Occasionally, what distracts the mind isn't a thought but a sensation or a sound. Try not to make judgments about what has happened; simply observe and move on.

- What we've just described is the fundamental practice of developing concentration. Concentration is the capacity to stay attentive to a single thing. Hindu yogis call this ability *ekgrata*, or one-pointedness.

- To train the mind to attain one-pointedness, we must learn to become aware of when the mind wanders from its anchor and then bring it back to its focal point. In learning to concentrate, we'll repeat this process over and over: The mind strays, and we return it to the breath.

- In doing so, we are doing more than simply learning to concentrate; we are also sharpening our awareness. The real challenge in the process of learning one-pointedness is to be attentive to the mind when it drifts. Because we are conditioned to be mindless, we're usually not aware of when we have lost our focus.

- When you notice your attention has gone astray—even if it takes 15 minutes before you realize it—just return your awareness to the breath. Don't criticize yourself. Being self-critical merely agitates the mind and thwarts the very serenity you're trying to realize.

- The important thing at this stage of the practice is not to prevent the mind from wandering away from its anchor, but simply to be aware of when it does. In other words, the real goal of this practice is awareness—not one-pointedness. Being able to concentrate our attention on one thing is simply a means for helping to attain greater consciousness of our experiences as they occur.

The Problem of Boredom

- As modern people, we have become accustomed to being constantly stimulated. Our minds crave novelty and excitement, and the ubiquity of technology has only exacerbated that hunger. When faced with the idea of paying attention to our breath for 15— or even 5—minutes, many of us recoil in horror. In fact, we expend a great deal of money and time trying to avoid being bored.

- Most of us think boredom is caused by our circumstances. We think the situation we find ourselves in is simply not interesting. The mindfulness traditions, on the other hand, regard boredom as the product of inattention. We get bored, in other words, when we withdraw our full awareness from whatever it is we are experiencing at the moment.

- Boredom isn't caused by our external circumstances but by our own mind. The antidote to boredom is paying complete attention. Rather than paying attention, though, most of us are inclined continually to seek out new mental stimulants to keep our minds occupied with trivialities.

- The practice of mindfulness encourages us to relinquish the craving for stimulation and simply be attentive to what is. Boredom itself can be interesting if you simply observe it patiently without judgment.

Complete Focus on the Breath

- When you can relinquish your fear of being bored and direct your full, receptive attention to your breath, you might be amazed at what you'll discover. You might notice what a pleasant sensation relaxed breathing brings. When you can be wholly engaged with the simple pleasure of breathing, you'll find yourself with a refined sense of completeness in that moment.

- Observing the breath might also teach you about our interconnectedness with the world. As we breathe, we are exchanging substances with the rest of reality. We take in the fresh oxygen produced by plant life and offer them the carbon dioxide they need. We depend on each other. Breathing also reminds us of our connectedness to our fellow human beings.

- Attending to the breath, we become acutely conscious of the passage of time. We can see that each breath is a fleeting event. This is something we know, of course, but careful observation reveals this fact in a vivid and profound way. You'll see that each breath is remarkably unique, just as each moment that contains it is unique.

- Focusing attention on the breath and returning to it when the mind strays constitutes the basic mindfulness practice. Before you proceed to the next lecture, you should practice this exercise. Everything else in this course is based on the simple discipline of attending to the breath, so it is important that you learn this practice and become as proficient as possible.

- Whether you decide to spend a few weeks—or even a few months—on the basic practice or choose to spend only a few minutes with it, try to incorporate sitting into your daily routine. Determine in advance how long you'd like to sit. Forty-five minutes is considered to be an optimal length of practice time, but like everything in this discipline, we take things in increments.

ekgrata: The term that Hindu yogis use for concentration, or one-pointedness.

mantra: A short saying or set of syllables that a meditator repeats to him- or herself.

Questions to Consider

1. What is the purpose of finding a focal point in the cultivation of mindfulness?

2. What makes the breath a particularly useful anchor?

Problems—Stepping-Stones to Mindfulness
Lecture 7

Problems are inevitable with this discipline; they should be expected. The problems you will necessarily face on this path are precisely the means that will help you progress along the way. Facing these difficulties in meditation will give us practice in confronting problems in the rest of our lives. In time, you'll see that what you thought were problems turn out to be stepping-stones to greater mindfulness. Remember that the most important aspect of any mediation practice is persistence. Never give up, and you will never fail.

Facing Difficulties with Courage

- Meditation is a microcosm of the rest of our life. Just as our lives are fraught with difficulties, so too is our meditation practice. Perhaps it is even more so, for in meditating we bring the manifold problems of our lives to sit with us while we face the special challenges that come with meditation itself.

- However, we should do more than just expect difficulties; we should welcome them. The real key to dealing with the problems we face in meditation is the attitude we take toward them. Often, our approach to life's difficulties is avoidance rather than confrontation.

- Only the complete acceptance of suffering leads to its end. To accept suffering, rather than flee from it, requires **courage**—the determination to look at difficulty straight in the eye. Courage is the fundamental attitude for facing problems.

- Although we sometimes equate courage and fearlessness, courage is not the absence of fear. Fear, in fact, is an essential component of courage. You cannot truly be courageous unless you can feel your fear fully. If you're able to stand your ground rather than averting your gaze or taking flight, that's courage.

- The very posture we assume as we meditate symbolizes the courage to which we aspire. When we determine to be still for 30 minutes, we're declaring our intention to look bravely at whatever our mind churns up without implementing our usual exit strategy.

- Facing difficulties is made easier by viewing them as opportunities to grow in awareness—to deepen our self-knowledge and our skills of compassion. We progress further by courageously meeting our difficulties than by not having them at all.

- As you reflect on the history of your life, you can see that the things that have contributed most to your personal development have been the trials you've faced and passed through.

- As we consider our difficulties in prospect, rather than in retrospect, the fears begin to well up in us. Perhaps we fear them because we think they'll overwhelm us, but the vast majority of our fears never materialize.

- Consider thinking of difficulties as merely things that require attention. Many times, there is nothing to do and nothing to solve—only something to watch, embrace, and learn from.

The Difficulties of Meditation

- There are certain difficulties associated with the discipline of meditation that are qualitatively no different than similar issues that arise when we're not meditating, but the specific aspects of meditation practice make them seem more prominent and more urgent.

- Pain may be the most common of these problems. Almost everyone has to adjust somehow to the physical discomfort that comes with meditation: Backs begin to ache, knees start to hurt, or legs go to sleep. Some of these discomforts will subside after continued practice, but some discomforts never go away.

- When you begin to experience pain, do what you can to eliminate it. If your clothes are too restrictive, change them. If you find sitting on a cushion too painful, try a chair. There is enough pain in life without adding more of it to mindfulness practice.

- There are certain discomforts that cannot be removed by altering our circumstances. However, meditation practice shows us that many of those discomforts can be mitigated by mindfulness.

Pain versus Suffering

- The mindfulness tradition understands pain as an unpleasant sensation. Because we comprise physical bodies, pain is inevitable. Suffering, however, is not the same as pain, although most of us equate the two.

- Suffering, as it's understood in mindfulness practice, is a mental and emotional response. It may or may not be associated with the sensation of pain. It's possible to suffer without pain, just as it's possible to feel pain without suffering.

- When the sensation of pain arises, we usually respond immediately with resistance, which is why pain and suffering are so closely associated in our minds. The slightest discomfort might cause us to wince and groan.

- Our minds may begin to go through any number of conditioned reactions: We feel a sense of unfairness, lodge a protest, and then fear sets in. Sometimes, fear turns to panic.

- Underlying all of these forms of resistance is the same belief: Pain shouldn't happen to us. That belief is a great source of our suffering. It can condition anger, fear, panic, and disillusionment.

- One way to reduce our suffering, then, is to align our minds with reality. Believing that pain shouldn't happen to us is delusional; it is inconsistent with the nature of the world. Rather than resist, we can be open to pain—to respond to it with compassionate mindfulness.

- It is possible, with sufficient training, to become an observer of our pain. Refining this technique can lessen one's suffering and may, in fact, lessen one's pain.

Dealing with Pain

- If physical discomfort appears as you meditate, allow the pain to become the object of your attention. Simply let the sensation itself provide the anchor for your awareness and become mindful of the pain as you would be of your breath. Watch the pain as you would watch your own inhalation and exhalation.

- Try to relax any tension or contraction of muscles surrounding the painful sensation. Observe the sensation with curiosity. Try to narrow your focus on the pain. Watch the pain change and move. If your focus is sharp enough, you can perceive the impermanent nature of pain. If you cannot stay focused on the sensation itself, direct your attention to how you're reacting to it.

- As you study your pain, you may find your resistance to it diminishing. It may continue to hurt, but you may suffer less because you are no longer struggling against it. With enough practice, you may find yourself simply watching pain as nothing more than a sensation, like any other.

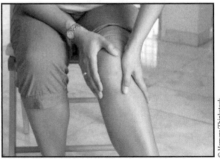
© Hemera/Thinkstock.

- In the early stages of practice, it is unrealistic to expect that this technique of

Most people have to adjust to the physical discomfort that comes with meditation, including backaches and knee pain.

observation will substantially lessen the suffering associated with severe pain, such as migraines. However, even that kind of pain can be ameliorated with mindfulness over time.

- Begin your work with pain on a minor discomfort, such as an itch. With itching, as with most sorts of discomforts, we reflexively try to stop it. The next time you get an itch as you're meditating, don't scratch. Instead, observe. Draw your attention to the itch and investigate it. Notice its qualities and its impermanence.

- After a few minutes of mindfulness, you may be able to watch the itch dissolve. If it doesn't, it's okay to scratch. When you scratch, however, just make sure you do so with complete awareness.

- As you continue working with little sensations, you will eventually become skilled enough to use these methods with more intense expressions of pain. People who endure chronic pain, in particular, have found the mindfulness approach to be helpful in ameliorating the sorts of pain that medicines are unable to treat.

Dealing with Strange Sensations

- As you meditate, you may feel a wide variety of strange things. These weird sensations probably occur all the time, but it's often only in meditation that we become sharply conscious of them. These sensations may be unpleasant, but they can just as well be pleasant or neutral. Such feelings are totally normal for meditation.

- Some of the commonly reported odd sensations include tingling in the arms, hands, legs, and feet; feeling the entire body becoming lighter, even to the extent of floating; and feeling the body—or parts of it, such as the hands—becoming larger.

- Unusual feelings can also involve vision and sound. If you meditate with your eyes closed, you may become distracted by the displays of lights on the insides of your eyelids. If you keep your eyes open, you might see odd patterns on the floor. If it is extremely quiet, you may find the silence deafening.

- If one of these strange sensations arises as you meditate, you should treat it like anything else: You should observe it and watch your reaction to it. If it is unpleasant, view it without aversion; if it is a pleasant sensation, view it without desire or attachment.

Dealing with Concentration

- Difficulty concentrating is hardly a problem unique to meditation, but it can be particularly vexing in this practice because so much in meditation concerns this skill.

- Focusing attention on the breath and returning to it when the mind wanders is the fundamental exercise for developing concentration and refining mindfulness. Over time, diligence with this practice can dramatically improve our ability to attain one-pointedness.

- If you're finding it hard to stay focused, first consider whether this difficulty might derive from experiences apart from meditation. For example, drowsiness is a potential threat to concentration that can often be dealt with before meditation begins by getting more sleep or eating less.

- While we can eliminate certain external circumstances that disrupt concentration, it is not always possible to do so. If it were, perhaps we wouldn't need to meditate at all.

- Just the ups and downs of a typical day can take their toll on the mind's capacity to remain attentive. If you cannot settle those disrupting influences before sit down to meditate, sit down anyway.

- There are several exercises you may use to regain and strengthen your concentration. First, simply try to take deeper breaths, inhaling and exhaling more forcibly than usual. This will heighten the sensation of breathing, giving your attention a more prominent object of focus. You can continue this exercise until you are able to stay more attentive to the breath.

- Another concentrative practice involves counting. There are a number of variations of this technique. When your attention is able to remain with the breath for longer periods, you can drop the counting. Counting itself can become a distraction, so use it only as a prop and then let it go.

Dealing with Discouragement

- Discouragement often comes when we meet with little success in coping with physical discomfort, weird sensations, and the inability to concentrate. Discouragement leads us to want to quit the practice altogether.

- There are some good ways to face discouragement in meditation—and they happen to be good ways to deal with it in the rest of our lives. The first way is to remind ourselves that the only way to fail at meditation is not to do it. The struggles we face and the ostensible "failures" we have are part of the process.

- The second thing you can do is to examine your experience of being disheartened. Look at it dispassionately. See where it comes from. Watch it come and go. Discouragement is just an emotion like any other. It will pass away.

- Sometimes the greatest problem we face in meditation is just sitting down. Regardless of how you feel about meditation at a particular moment, you should just do it anyway—no argument, no excuses. If that strategy fails, try to remind yourself of the many benefits to be gained by developing your mindfulness.

- Usually, any aversive feelings toward the practice evaporate after a few minutes once you sit down. Once you settle into your meditation, you can begin to explore the source of your aversion. You'll probably discover some sort of fear lurking underneath your resistance, which you can meet with courage.

Important Term

courage: The ability to accept suffering rather than flee from it; the determination to look at difficulty straight in the eye.

Questions to Consider

1. How do you define courage? Why is courage important in living a full life? What aspects of your life could most benefit from the application of the virtue of courage?

2. What role does fear play in your life? What fears restrict your life the most?

Body—Attending to Our Physical Natures
Lecture 8

You can consider the body scan as one element in the practice of self-compassion. By carefully watching the various components of your body with curiosity and openness, you are extending to your own physical nature the same compassionate attentiveness you might offer to a good friend. Sometimes we find it harder to be kind to ourselves than we do to others. That difficulty reflects an estrangement within us. By giving compassionate attention to our bodies, we come closer to healing that alienation.

The Body Scan

- Mindfulness of the breath is not the only form of meditation in this tradition. Another kind of practice that builds upon the basics is known as a body scan. Because this technique uses some of the same skills as meditation that is focused on breathing, it can serve as a way to augment and support it.

- Some instructors, in fact, use the body scan as the foundational practice for teaching mindfulness. In becoming proficient with both techniques, you may find that you prefer one to the other, or you might discover them equally helpful in fostering moment-to-moment awareness.

- In the body scan, we'll take the same skill of directing attention that is used in the practice of attending to the breath and use it to focus our awareness on various aspects of our body. This operation gives us the opportunity to build up the skill of concentration by systematically surveying the body using focused attention.

- This process is similar to the way we can shine a flashlight to help illumine an object in the dark. The light brings the object of our choosing into relief while what surrounds it remains darkened. If we wish, we can move the light to other areas to bring them into view. This is the way focused attention operates.

- This practice does more than simply strengthen our concentrative abilities; it also helps acquaint us with our own bodies. Just as we are strangers to the operation of our own minds, we're often strangers to our physical entities. The body scan fosters awareness of our bodies by allowing us to feel its sensations on a part-by-part basis.

- The body scan also has the great benefit of promoting relaxation— perhaps even to a greater extent than sitting meditation. In fact, you can become so relaxed using this technique that you may fall asleep, which is fine. However, to gain the greatest benefit from this exercise, you should be well rested before you begin.

- Like meditation on breathing, the body scan can be practiced alone, but to learn this particular form of meditation, it is especially helpful to be guided through it in a step-by-step format. Once you have been led through a body scan, you can conduct it on your own at any time.

- You will need to allocate about 20 minutes for the entire body scan meditation exercise that follows, and you will need to have access to a quiet place free from distractions and interruptions.

- The body scan can be practiced in either a sitting or lying position, and you should try both postures at some point to see which best suits you. For our introduction to this exercise, however, we will use the lying position because many people find this posture easier. If you're a practitioner of hatha yoga, you may recognize the position as *shavasana*, the corpse pose.

- Before we begin, you'll need to be wearing comfortable, loose-fitting clothes, and you'll need some sort of padding to provide a little cushioning if you'll be lying on the bare floor. A lightly padded but firm surface is best. You might also want to use a thin pillow to cushion your head.

The Body Scan in Practice

- When you're prepared, lie down on your back in a supine position— with your face upward. If you want to relieve some of the tension in your back, place a pillow or blanket under your knees to elevate them slightly.

- Allow your shoulders, middle back, lower back, and hips to settle into the surface on which you're lying. Try to move your shoulder blades together slightly to allow your arm sockets to move toward the ground. Gently coax your shoulders toward your feet. Allow your hands to be open, palms up. Let your feet fall open, away from each other. Allow your head to feel heavy against the ground. Take a few deep breaths and become attentive to the inhalation and exhalation as the breath returns to its natural rhythm. Focus your attention on the sensation of breathing at the nostrils or with the rising and falling of the abdomen.

- If your mind begins to drift and dwell on thoughts or sounds, lightly return it to the sensation of breathing. Concentrate your efforts on being fully present to your experience. With each exhalation, feel your body become heavier and more relaxed.

- Now, direct your attention to your feet: Let go of any tension you may feel, and allow your feet to relax as you breathe out. Pay attention to your legs. Release any tension you may feel in this area of your body, and let your legs relax as you breathe out. Be aware of your arms and hands. If you feel any tension, let it go; allow your arms and hands to relax as you breathe out.

- Direct your awareness to your abdomen, chest, and back. Let go of any tension you may feel, and relax this area as you breathe out. Bring your attention to your neck, shoulders, and head. Allow any tightness you may feel to dissolve, and relax these parts of your body as you breathe out.

- Now that you have settled into position, allow yourself to feel your whole body as a single organism; continue to breathe naturally, letting yourself become deeply relaxed as you do.

- Now, focus your awareness on your scalp and the area on the top of your head. Allow your attention to move systematically throughout this area. Be open and inquisitive. Try to feel the sensation in that area of your body as it is. Be aware of the quality of the sensation. You may feel tightness, tingling, pressure, stiffness, or nothing in particular. If there is no sensation, just notice. Whatever the sensation, just permit it to be what it is, without judgment. Now, let go of those sensations in this part of the body and continue to breathe naturally.

- Now, bring your attention to your face: For a few moments, focus on your forehead and temples and become aware of any sensation in this area. Allow your attention to survey this part of your body with openness, simply accepting what is there. Note the quality of those sensations and relinquish them.

- Direct your awareness to your eyes and the area surrounding your eyes, and continue to note and accept the sensations you feel. If your mind has begun to wander from its attentiveness to the body, gently return it to where it should be.

- Now, allow your attention to move to other parts of your face, focusing on the nose, cheeks, and mouth. Then, become mindful of your chin, jaw, and ears—all the while observing and accepting the sensations in these areas as they are.

- Move your awareness now to the back of your head and to the top of your neck. Notice if there is tension, tingling, stiffness, or no sensation at all. Just take note of whatever you feel and let that be sufficient. Be aware and open to whatever you sense. Allow your attention to move down your neck and throat and to the top of your shoulders. Feel every aspect of these areas.

- Now, bring your awareness to your arms. Feel the inside and outside of your upper arms—noticing any sensations—as you move your attention down to the elbows, forearms, wrists, and then hands. Survey each of your fingers. Carefully try to feel every sensation, every bit of tension or pressure, tingling or lightness. Examine if the area feels warm or cool—or has no sensation at all. Don't struggle with what you feel; simply have a caring interest in what is happening. Try to be fully attentive to your experience.

- Now, relinquish your attention to your arms and hands, and direct it to the top of the chest, noticing any sensation as you move along. From the chest, follow the ribs to the upper back and to the shoulder blades. The sensation may be pleasurable, unpleasant, or simply absent. Accept whatever is there with gentleness and compassion.

- Next, let your attention move down the spine to your lower back, and then bring your awareness to the abdomen. Take a moment to feel yourself breathe, as your belly and lower back expand and contract with each inhalation and exhalation. Feel the subtle movements of the breath, noticing the slight pressure of your clothing as you breathe. In this area of your body, you may feel sensations in your internal organs as they function to keep you alive.

- Allow your awareness to move to your hips and groin. If your mind has begun to drift, gently refocus your attention on this part of the body. Sense the physical impressions in this area and note their qualities. Accept each sensation as it is; just observe and move on.

- Bring your attention to your upper legs. First, observe the way the muscles and skin of your inner thighs feel, and then do the same for the muscles and skin of your outer thighs. Slowly scan downward to your knees. Feel each and every sensation. Be aware of everything, and continue to breathe. If your mind has wandered, escort it back to where you want it to be.

- Continue to move your awareness down your legs, shifting attention to your shins and then your calves, noticing any tension or tingling—any pleasant or unpleasant feelings. Be mindful as you give attention to your ankles and heels, to the tops and soles of your feet, and finally to your toes. Try to bring your awareness to each of your toes, feeling whatever sensation might be perceptible.

- Now, allow your awareness to encompass your entire body as a whole. Take time to feel the sensation of being alive in this moment. You may feel deeply relaxed and suffused with a sense of well-being and peacefulness. You can return to this peacefulness at any time.

- When you are ready to end the meditation, slowly move your fingers and toes—and then your arms and legs. Open your eyes and gently move the other parts of your body. Then, very carefully, roll over to one side and use your arms and hands to bring yourself to a sitting position.

Variations on the Body Scan

- Now that you have become acquainted with the basic features of the body scan, feel free to vary the practice in ways you find most beneficial. As mentioned, the body scan can be performed in the sitting posture or in a standing pose. You can conduct the practice at a faster or slower pace, or you can scan your body from toes to head or right to left or left to right. The variations are many, and you should determine for yourself which possibilities you find most valuable in promoting awareness and relaxation.

Important Term

shavasana: This position is known as the corpse pose and is practiced in hatha yoga.

1. How do you imagine the relationship between the body and mind?

2. In what ways does the body scan augment the practice of sitting meditation?

Mind—Working with Thoughts
Lecture 9

W e may not be able to control particular thoughts, but we can influence the conditioned mind that gives rise to particular thoughts. We can prepare a fertile mental soil that increases the likelihood of germinating wholesome, skillful ideas and decreases the likelihood of growing distracting ones—but such a mind must be tended with a watchful eye. Unwholesome thoughts grow fast and wild and leech vital nutrients from the thoughts that are conducive to our freedom and happiness.

The Tamed Mind

- The mind is a double-edged sword: It is capable of doing us great benefit as well as great injury. Naturally, we want to cultivate our mental processes in such a way that we maximize the mind's capacity for doing good and minimize its tendencies for causing suffering. The skills we refine as we develop moment-to-moment awareness in sitting meditation are the same used in shaping the mind to function in more wholesome ways.

- As we've observed both casually and in formal meditation, the untamed mind tends to operate in a rather haphazard way, bounding from thought to thought with little or no apparent prompting or direction. The mind seems to have a mind of its own. Thus, it might appear that our thoughts are thoroughly beyond our control—that we have no choice about the kinds of things that drift across our minds.

- Although thoughts may seem to come out of the blue, they are, in fact, conditioned by previous patterns of thought. The thoughts that our mind produces now have been shaped by its history of thinking.

- Recent neuroscientific research has shown that routine patterns of thought make incremental but substantial changes in the way the brain is structured and the way the mind functions. These structural alterations make the brain more effective at doing what it is asked to do.

- If we habitually think in certain ways, the mind becomes more adept at those patterns of thought. Thus, as the concept of conditioning suggests, wholesome thoughts create a propensity for more wholesome thoughts, and unwholesome thoughts predispose the mind to produce more unwholesome thoughts.

- Fortunately, we can use this dynamic principle to our advantage. While we may not be in conscious control of each and every thought, meditation practice shows us that we can choose which thoughts to entertain and develop and which to observe and release. In this manner, we can influence the kinds of thoughts we are likely to produce in the future.

- In the meditation practices we've discussed so far, our practice of releasing thoughts has been indiscriminate. We've been training the mind to drop any thought as soon as we become aware of it, without regard to its content or quality. The purpose of this particular practice is to reinforce our ability to focus and be attentive.

- When we have become sufficiently proficient at using these techniques, we can add another component to the practice that will enable us to manage our thinking more consciously. In this new method, we will endeavor not only to become aware of thoughts as they arise, but also to identify the kind of thoughts we are having. Once identified, we can make conscious choices about how we will handle them.

The Unskilled Mind

- Because of our conditioning, the great majority of our thoughts are not conducive to our well-being. In the mindless state, our thoughts can be highly critical of others—and of ourselves. When you attend carefully to the quality of your thoughts, you might easily conclude that most of them serve little constructive purpose in our lives.

- Because of the mind's overproduction of unwholesome thoughts, it redounds to our benefit to be able to respond appropriately and immediately when such thoughts arise. Doing this, of course, requires sharp attention and the capacity to discern wholesome from unwholesome thoughts.

- Unfortunately, the unskilled mind finds this difficult to do. Just as the untrained mind has difficulty even knowing when it is absorbed in thought, it finds it hard to know when a thought is edifying or corrosive. Often, the undisciplined mind even fails to appreciate the importance of this distinction.

- The mindfulness tradition offers very specific ways of identifying harmful thoughts and enables us to see why they are problematic. According to this tradition, an unwholesome thought is one that is not conducive to freedom and happiness but, rather, promotes suffering. Conversely, wholesome thoughts diminish suffering and foster happiness and freedom.

Unwholesome Thoughts

- Unwholesome thoughts may be recognized by certain telltale traits. Specifically, unwholesome thoughts—which we can also call unskillful thoughts—are connected to selfish desire, hatred, or delusion.

- Thoughts associated with selfish desire are predicated on our voracious appetite for pleasure. An unwholesome thought of this sort may prompt us to act or speak in a way that provides us with momentary gratification.

- Whereas thoughts based on selfish desire draw us toward an act that we believe will give us pleasure, thoughts associated with hatred repel us from people or situations we think will cause us pain or make us feel uncomfortable.

- Deluded thoughts are at odds with reality and result from our failure to see ourselves and the world as they really are. On the basis of delusion, we can generate grandiose thoughts about our own importance or our own worthlessness, or we can somehow come to believe that we are immune to the vicissitudes to which everyone else is subject.

- It requires skill, of course, to recognize these unskillful thoughts, and ultimately, it takes knowing ourselves very well—the kind of self-knowledge that comes only with ruthless honesty and dispassionate observation.

- To give you some practice at identifying unskillful thoughts, try this simple exercise the next time you meditate or sit in the park. Whenever you catch your mind drifting in its usual haphazard way, take a moment to examine the character of the thought that has captured your attention.

- The great danger of entertaining any thought that arises from selfish desire, hatred, and delusion is its eventual effects on the shape of our minds. Even the thoughts that remain confined to the interior of our skulls can proliferate, generating habits of thought that form our personality and character.

Attending to Unwholesome Thoughts

- The mindfulness tradition offers a variety of very practical ways to assist us in disempowering unwholesome thoughts and relaxing their corrosive effects on the mind. They're all forms of relinquishment, and they're all dependent on our ability to recognize an unwholesome thought when it arises.

Replacement

- In some ways, replacement is the simplest and most effective method of disarming a harmful thought. When an unwholesome thought arises, we immediately supplant it with a wholesome one. The

Buddha likened this method to the way a woodworker might knock out a coarse peg with a fine one.

© Comstock/Thinkstock.

- This approach is most effective when the unskillful thought is replaced by a skillful one that directly counteracts it. Thoughts based

Initially, the practice of replacing unwholesome thoughts with wholesome ones may seem artificial in situations such as road rage.

on selfish desire, for example, can be substituted by thoughts about the impermanence of the object of desire. Thoughts grounded in hatred can be replaced with notions of friendliness and compassion. Finally, thoughts founded on delusion can be overcome by thoughts based in reality.

- Initially, the technique of replacing thoughts may seem awkward and artificial, but if you act in a certain way over time—even when it doesn't feel authentic—those actions will eventually begin to feel and be real and genuine.

Reflecting on Results

- We can also contemplate the consequences of the unwholesome thought by reflecting on the results. When unwholesome thoughts arise, we think about the effects of holding these unwise notions. Consider the kind of person you become when you entertain and foster a particular unwholesome thought. If mind shapes our experience, then our thoughts have ineluctable consequences.

- Follow the trajectory of an unwholesome thought. It's not even necessary to reflect on the consequences of acting on these thoughts; you can simply think about having your mind packed with such ideas.

- The Buddha compares the unwholesome thought to a snake or animal carcass around the neck of a well-dressed person. Such a thought, he argues, is unbecoming to a wise and compassionate human being. When the unskillful thought appears, don't denounce it; just let it go, reminding yourself that it is not reflection of who you truly are.

Redirecting

- Redirecting is simply diverting attention away from the unwholesome thought to something more beneficial. The Buddha compared this technique to averting one's gaze to avoid staring at certain objects.

- In sitting meditation, when the mind has been distracted by thought, we simply escort the attention back to the breath. Thus, our practice of meditation strengthens our ability to employ this technique.

- Redirecting attention relies on the impermanence of reality to work. We're all aware that everything in the world will change and pass away. That thought usually occasions within us a feeling of sadness or melancholy. However, the impermanence of reality can be a source of comfort and happiness when we accept it, and we have to be constantly reminded to accept it.

- Redirecting attention helps us to accept the impermanence of the world and to use that fact to our benefit. Thoughts, like everything else, pass away. To maintain a thought, we have to renew it, which is why we have to be reminded of life's transience. Of course, if we renew the unwholesome thought, it will arise again, at which point we escort our attention elsewhere. Eventually, by redirecting attention, the unwholesome thought will lose its power and fade.

- Redirecting attention need not use the breath as its anchor; any wholesome thought or activity can suffice. Far better to keep oneself diligently engaged with wholesome activity lest the straying mind comes to dwell in greed, aversion, and delusion.

Reconstructing

- Reconstructing involves analyzing the formation of the unskillful thought. In reflecting on results, we contemplate the forward trajectory of an unwholesome thought, considering its consequences for the future. With reconstructing, on the other hand, we examine the antecedents that have given rise to the unwholesome notion.

- Through the process of reconstructing, we can begin to examine the assumptions supporting a particular belief. This allows us to see how unwholesome thoughts can be rooted in untenable assumptions that we make about the things that will make us happy, and it allows us to examine those assumptions more rationally.

- When we've analyzed the root causes of envy enough times, we come to recognize a peculiar pattern of unskillful thinking that most of us routinely practice. It's a manner of thought strongly encouraged by our competitive culture.

- The mindfulness tradition calls restructuring "comparing mind," which is the insidious habit of seeing how we measure up to other people. Our culture is obsessed with it and, in a sense, thrives on it.

- The foremost disadvantage of comparing mind is the unnecessary suffering it causes: We not only feel bad about ourselves, but we often begin to wish ill upon the person we envy—sometimes to the point where we take steps to realize those wishes.

- Whether we judge ourselves favorably or unfavorably, the practice of comparing mind is unwholesome. It causes us harm, expends our precious mental energy, and erodes our relationships with others.

- Although it is generally unskillful, there are times when comparing mind can be used skillfully, but doing so is an advanced practice that requires great wisdom. For most of us, however, certainly in the early stages of mindfulness practice, it is a habit that is best acknowledged and then relinquished.

Questions to Consider

1. As you meditate, try to identify patterns of unwholesome, or unskillful, thinking. What kinds of negative thoughts seem to dominate your thinking life?

2. Which techniques to deal with unwholesome thoughts work best for you?

Walking—Mindfulness While Moving
Lecture 10

We often overlook the tremendous potential of the simplest things in our lives. Consider walking. It's something virtually all of us do every day of our lives, yet how much attention do we even give to this basic aspect of our existence? The vast majority of our walking is spent in mindlessness, eager to get from one place to another with nary a thought about how we're getting there. It's quite a metaphor for the way we live our lives.

Walking Meditation

- Although most of us give little consideration to the activity of walking, some of the most thoughtful among us have been keenly aware of its importance. Walking need not be just a way to move our brains around; walking can help improve the way those brains work.

- Being physically calm, as we have observed, helps foster the mental tranquility necessary for moment-to-moment awareness. However, bodily stillness is not essential to mindfulness; it merely helps promote it, especially for those who are in the initial stages of learning the practice.

- Walking meditation shares the same goal as all practices in this tradition—that of gaining deeper awareness—but it approaches that objective in a different and complementary way from the techniques that involve physical stillness. In this way, walking meditation provides a balance to the other practices.

- Many practitioners have come to prefer walking mindfulness to the motionless forms of meditation because walking practice can be more versatile than sitting: It doesn't require a particular setting or equipment, such as a chair or cushion.

- Before you try this form of meditation during a stroll in the park or on the way from the car to the office, it's a good idea to get some experience in a special setting that is free from distractions and hazards so that you can master the basic technique.

- Like sitting meditation, walking has a number of variations that you can explore to help you design the practice that is most effective for you. Experiment with these variations to determine which techniques best sharpen your awareness.

Preparing for Walking Meditation

- To begin the practice of walking meditation, you must first find a suitable location. You can walk within the privacy of your own home, your own backyard, or any other space free from dangers and distractions. The fresh air of the outdoors, of course, has much to recommend it.

- The space for walking doesn't need to be large, but you will be walking back and forth on this space. You'll start at one end, walk to the other end, turn around, and walk the other way—repeating this many times.

- The space doesn't need to be demarcated in any way; you can simply set the boundaries in your imagination. The surface of the walkway only needs to be level and stable. If you walk barefoot—which is a very pleasant thing to do—just make sure the walking surface will not endanger your feet.

- Like sitting meditation, there is no single best time for practicing walking meditation. If you are able to do so, however, walking just before or just after sitting meditation is beneficial; walking and sitting alternately has a synergistic effect on mindfulness. Whereas sitting meditation after a meal can lead to drowsiness, research suggests that a gentle walk after eating can be healthy and invigorating.

- Before you begin, make sure you're wearing comfortable clothing, appropriate to your environment. Divest yourself of needless sources of distraction or discomfort, such as cell phones or music players. You may want to stretch a bit to loosen and relax your muscles. Do whatever is necessary to maximize your sense of freedom.

Walking Meditation in Practice

- When you're ready to start your mediation, take your place at one end of your walkway. Stand tall with your spine upright and your shoulders relaxed, letting your arms hang naturally by your sides. Keep your chin level with the ground. Relax your jaw and smile slightly. Take a few slow, deep breaths.

- Using a body scan, briefly survey the different areas of your body from the feet to the top of your head, releasing any tension as you do. For a few moments, simply stand there and observe the sensations of your body. Take a moment to appreciate your surroundings and the feel and fragrance of the air.

© Comstock/Thinkstock.

It may be beneficial to engage in basic walking practice outdoors with fresh air.

- Pay special attention to the sensations at the bottom of your feet. If you're barefoot, allow yourself to completely feel the qualities of your walking surface. Wiggle your toes a bit to let them sense the textures under your feet.

- As you prepare to walk, remind yourself of your intention to be mindful during this exercise, just as you do at the beginning of sitting meditation. Now, focus your vision on the ground about five or six feet in front of you, but don't gaze at anything in particular. You'll keep your eyes open during the entire meditation.

- You can place your hands in front of you or behind. If you hold them in front, you may put one hand in the other, as in sitting meditation. If you put them behind you, let one hand clasp the other and allow them to rest against the back. You can also allow the arms to remain at your sides and swing slightly as you move.

- Now, begin to walk, using small, careful steps. Mindfully, lift your right foot, move it forward, and place it on the ground a few inches beyond the toes of your left foot. Then, allow your weight to shift onto your right leg, and mindfully lift your left foot. Then, move it and place it on the ground a few inches beyond the toes of your right foot. Shift the weight of your body forward onto your left leg. Repeat.

- It's basic walking, of course, except with greater attention to the experience. At first, walking with attentiveness may feel awkward. Beginning practitioners sometimes even lose their balance because they're trying to be conscious of what is ordinarily an unconscious process. The awkwardness will dissipate as you become accustomed to the pace and deliberate style of the practice.

- As you move, be sure to retain an upright posture. Many people walk improperly, allowing their head and upper torso to lead their body. To maintain a correct carriage as you walk, imagine the rest of your body being led forward by the belly rather than by the head and chest.

- Initially, you may find it helpful to coordinate your movements with your breath. On the inhalation, you can lift and move the foot, and as you exhale, you can place the foot and shift your weight. You'll probably discover, however, that your breath and bodily movements will fall into a natural, synchronized rhythm after a while.

- This natural rhythm will allow your mind and body to relax. When you sense this harmony, you can withdraw your attention from the breath. Unlike sitting, in walking practice, we allow the breath to fade into the background and place our attention on other bodily sensations.

Focusing Awareness

- There are several places where you may focus your awareness. Some instructors recommend attending to the legs and feet while silently labeling the three parts of each step—lifting, moving, and placing. You may find this technique helpful for your practice, but only use it in the initial stages of learning.

- An alternative method involves focusing your awareness on the sensations of your feet as they make contact with the ground. This technique is most effective when you're walking barefoot. Due to a high concentration of nerve endings, the bottoms of the feet are among the most sensitive areas of the body. Consequently, they provide an excellent anchor for the attention.

- If you find yourself distracted by a thought or an emotion, you can gently return attention to the soles of the feet. If you find it helpful, you can pause to refocus your awareness and then resume your walk. As in other forms of meditation, allow your mind to be relaxed and focused.

- A third technique is to direct your awareness to the sensation of your body as a whole. Rather concentrate on a particular part, try to gain a sense of the body as a single organism. Be open and attentive to whatever experiences come your way. This method is especially useful when you want to practice walking mindfully at a faster pace.

- Regardless of the technique you choose, your objective is to keep your attention on each moment, as time moves from one instant to the next. If at any moment you wish to stop and enjoy your environment—to watch the leaves fall or to listen to a sparrow's chirp—you should feel free to do so.

Completing the Walk

- When you reach the end of your path, come to a complete stop. Stand still and observe your whole body. If you wish, you can do a brief body scan or simply take a few moments to enjoy the sensation of being alive. You can walk for as long or as short a period as you like, but 30 minutes is a good time for beginners and experienced practitioners.

- When you are ready, begin slowly and mindfully to turn around 180 degrees. Stop your turn when you're facing the other end of the walkway. Once again, set your intention to be mindful during the next segment and begin again.

- Once you've become accustomed to the basic skills of mindful walking, you're free to vary the practice in ways that you find meaningful. As you walk, you might recite a **_gatha_**, a short verse from the Buddhist tradition that focuses the mind on a wholesome thought.

- Walking practice can also be modified to emphasize our full attentiveness in the present moment. One way to use walking for this purpose is to stop at each step and bring your complete attention to that moment before taking another step. By so doing, you're reminding yourself that life is a series of present moments.

- Walking can also be a way of imagining letting go. With each pace, you can envision leaving your anxieties and worries behind and taking a fresh step into a new moment. It's important to remember that although you're walking, you're not going anywhere. Walking meditation has no destination but awareness.

Being Mindful Anywhere

- Anytime you walk, you can be mindful. Your pace will probably be more brisk than the formal practice, and you'll probably find it most helpful to stay aware of your entire body as it moves, rather than focusing on the feet. Rather than thinking about your destination, stay focused on the act of walking.

- Anytime is a good time to walk mindfully, but this practice is especially helpful when you get angry. The next time you're taken with anger, try to walk mindfully. You'll discover that it cools the fires of rage.

- Another variation on the practice involves using a contemplative tool that has regained popularity among many Christians in recent years. **Labyrinths** are intricate structures or patterns that define a pathway; they have been found in a wide range of cultures throughout history and assume a variety of different shapes.

- A labyrinth should not be confused with a **maze**, which is a kind of puzzle with many pathway options. You can get lost in a maze, and the goal is to find a way out. A labyrinth, however, has only a single route. It has twists and turns like a maze—but no branches offering alternative paths.

Important Terms

gatha: A short verse from the Buddhist tradition that focuses the mind on a wholesome thought.

labyrinth: Intricate structures or patterns that define a pathway; it has twists and turns but only a single route.

maze: A kind of puzzle with many pathway options; one can get lost in a maze, and the goal is to find a way out.

1. Why do you think philosophers such as Nietzsche, Kant, and Thoreau considered walking essential to their creativity?

2. Do sitting and walking meditation affect your mind differently? What are the differences? Which style do you prefer and why?

Consuming—Watching What You Eat
Lecture 11

Mindful eating is a way to enjoy one of the most pleasurable, yet one of the most ordinary, things we do. It's also a practice that allows us to discover—or perhaps rediscover—many wonderful things that happen right under our noses and within our bodies. Mindful eating helps us attend to our body's inner wisdom and to our natural capacity for compassion and gratitude. It also helps us appreciate our place in the greater web of life.

Eating with Mindfulness

- Like walking, consuming our food and drink is a profoundly ordinary experience whose depth is usually overlooked. Most of us, most of the time, devour mindlessly, missing out on what is potentially one of the most satisfying experiences we can have.

- To introduce you to mindful eating, we will mindfully eat a tangerine. You can perform this exercise with any kind of food, but this meditation is designed specifically for tangerines. As you'll see shortly, the practice means nothing without your participation.

Mindfully Eating a Tangerine

- First, find a quiet, well-lit location where you can sit comfortably, free from distractions. You can do this at the kitchen table, on the sofa, or in your meditation space.

- Take the tangerine in your hands and close your eyes. Allow your fingers and palms to touch the fruit's surface, carefully attending to your sensations. Take your time. Notice its shape. Feel it as if you were going to draw a picture of the fruit afterward. Observe the irregularities, the bumps and crevices, the curves and flat areas. Examine the texture of the skin.

- Now, hold the tangerine up to your nostrils. Feel it with your nose and lips and the area between them—called the philtrum. Move it around a bit and sniff. Notice your reaction to the citrusy fragrance.

- Open your eyes and hold the tangerine about 12 inches away from them, allowing your gaze to focus on the fruit. Observe the subtle shadings of color, noting the reflection of light on the surface. Find the place where the fruit was attached to the tree. These tiny details make this tangerine different from every other tangerine in the world.

Mindfully eating a tangerine can be a wonderful experience that deepens your awareness of the world.

- Ponder for a few moments how this tangerine came to be in your hand. Think of the tree that produced it. Imagine how many generations of tangerine trees preceded the tree from which this particular fruit came. Think of the person who planted the tree and the people who tended it. Consider all the sunshine, air, and water that were necessary to nourish that tree and produce this fruit.

- It took many years, many hands, and many physical elements for this tangerine to be with you at just this moment. And shortly, part of this fruit will become part of you, and all those years, the work of all those people and insects, and all the sunshine and water will become part of you as well.

- Now, we'll take the fruit and begin to open it. Break the skin with your thumbnail. Smell it again. The fragrance is more intense and

81

richer. Continue to press your nail into the skin and slowly peel it back. Keep it as close to your eyes as you find comfortable.

- Feel your thumb exerting pressure on the fruit, tearing into the soft flesh. Look at the yellow-white pulp underneath. See the texture and the shades of color. Notice how the skin and pulp pull away from the fruit as your thumb slides deeper within. See the strings of pulp that cling to the tangerine sections.

- Observe the interesting shapes the peeling forms as you continue to remove it from the edible part within. Carefully finish detaching the skin and pulp, studying each detail. Feel the sensation of moisture on your thumb and fingers. See how some parts of the peeling can be more easily removed than others.

- For a few moments, hold the tangerine close to your ear as you peel. Listen to the sound of the skin tearing away from the fleshy part. When you have completely separated the peeling from the flesh, take a minute to look at and smell the skin before putting it aside.

- Now, take the edible flesh and observe. Notice the colors, the textures, the many crescent-shaped sections of the fruit. See how rough the surface appears and the filaments of pulp sticking to it. Begin to break the cluster of sections in half. Hear the sounds of separation and watch as the sections try to cling to one another. Notice the pulpy part in the center.

- Gently remove one section of the cluster. Observe the patterns on the section's translucent skin. Peel away a bit of skin to reveal the orange, juicy flesh. The section comprises even more parts within. See how tightly packed they are—how nicely arrayed—each part about to burst.

- Take the section and place it in your mouth, letting it rest on your tongue. Don't bite it just yet. Close your eyes. Let your tongue examine the fruit. Use your tongue to move the tangerine section to your molars and softly bite into it, but don't bite completely through. Just chew the flesh slightly to allow the fruit to release its juices. Let the liquid flow from the fruit and swish it around in your mouth a bit. Taste it.

- Now, continue to chew slowly and thoroughly. Then, allow the fruit to slide down your throat and swallow. For a few seconds, concentrate on the lingering sensations in your mouth. Notice how the sensations that were so intense just a few moments ago are now fading away. Examine your response to that impermanence.

- When you're ready, pick up another slice and repeat the process, all the while concentrating on your sensations and reactions—trying to savor the experience without judgment or evaluation. Do this for each section of the tangerine until it's gone. Pause between each section. Don't pick up another section until you have completely finished with the one that's in your mouth.

Eating Mindfully as a Habit

- The value of this exercise is to reveal the possibilities available to us for using the ordinary experience of eating to deepen our awareness and act in more wholesome ways. Perhaps it would be great to eat this way all the time, but for many of us, that's not practical. We can, however, incorporate some of the methods and principles of tangerine meditation into our daily lives in relatively painless—but very meaningful—ways.

- First, let me suggest that you set a goal to practice mindful eating during one meal each week. This is a modest beginning, and as you start to see the benefits, you may want to have mindful meals with greater frequency. You'll also begin to notice how the practice of mindfulness while eating begins to affect all of your eating experiences.

- After committing yourself to a regular practice, decide if you'd like to observe it alone or with others. Eating with others provides additional richness to the experience when they are also committed to the practice. Although no one says a word, having a mindful supper with friends and family can strengthen the intimacy of these relationships.

- Whether you choose to eat alone or with others, the practice of mindful eating really begins before the meal starts, as you choose and prepare your food. If you dine with company, it's an enriching practice to include them in the preparation phase.

Choosing the Menu

- It's important to give careful thought to the menu. The principal reason we eat is to nourish our bodies and minds, so making wise choices about the food that will ultimately become us is essential. The mindfulness tradition doesn't specify a particular kind of diet; it only encourages us to consume food and drink that will keep us healthy and contribute to our moment-to-moment awareness.

- Knowing what is wholesome food and what's not, however, isn't always easy. Almost daily, the media reports the shifting opinions about this or that food item. For now, we can only say that mindfulness practice entails using our best wisdom and the knowledge we have available to choose the most wholesome foods.

- Being conscious of what we eat also involves awareness of how food gets to our table. Unless we grow all our own food, we probably have little idea about where most of what we eat comes from or how it is produced.

Cooks everywhere—from gourmet chefs to mothers and fathers—help sustain life and bring happiness.

© Digital Vision/Thinkstock.

- We exist in a complex web of life. How we sustain our own life has a profound effect on the rest of the biosphere of which we are part. Today, we are becoming more aware that how we get our food affects the greater world in which we live.

- As an exercise in mindfulness, investigate where some of your food comes from—or at least give some thought to the source of your food before you eat it, as we did in our tangerine meditation. If you're able, consider gardening, if you don't already.

The Gift of Eating

One day, a man was strolling across a field when suddenly he came face-to-face with a hungry tiger. Instinctively, he bolted, and the tiger, just as instinctively, ran after him. Knowing he had no chance to outrun the animal, the man jumped down a cliff and grabbed hold of a vine growing on the side. He looked up and saw the tiger just above him, licking his chops. He looked down below to the bottom of the cliff, where another hungry tiger was waiting for him to fall. Then, two mice—one black, the other white—began to nibble away at the vine. Just then, the man saw a juicy wild strawberry growing in the crag. He reached for it. It was incredibly delicious!

Zen Buddhists have told this parable for ages as a way to express the inexpressible essence of Zen. Like the hapless man in the story, our fate is inescapable. The jaws of death await us all, sooner or later, as time itself gnaws away at our lifeline.

That being the case, why complain or despair? Why not become fully alive to the moment we've been offered? Why not reach out and savor the wild strawberry? Every day of our lives, these moments are given to us as gifts, but we usually return them unopened. Eating, as the parable suggests, is one of these gifts.

- When the food has been bought and the menu set, you can make preparation itself a mindful practice. Work in a quiet, clean, distraction-free environment. Enjoy the sensual nature of your experience. Notice colors, textures, aromas, and tastes.

- Think about how your actions are part of the greater web of life. Reflect on the fact that other beings have given up their lives to sustain yours. If you're cooking for others—or even just for yourself—remember that what you are doing is an act of compassion. You're helping to sustain life and bring happiness.

Eating a Meal in Mindfulness

- When you are ready to begin the meal, make sure the location is quiet and uncluttered. An appropriate beginning to a mindfulness meal could be a few words encouraging reflection on the purpose of eating, the process by which the food has come to table, and the fact that many in the world are malnourished. Depending on your personal beliefs, these words may or may not make mention of God.

- When grace is concluded, the meal may begin. Eating the entire meal in silence helps create an environment conducive to moment-to-moment awareness. If you have company, eating in silence may seem awkward at first, but most people quickly become used to it.

- Eating a meal in mindfulness follows the same principles as the tangerine meditation, with just a few variations and additional options. You will, of course, eat slowly and attentively, trying to experience the richness of the moment. It will be most helpful to vary your usual eating experience to break the habits of mindless eating.

- Eat your meal at a leisurely pace, and be keenly attentive to your body to know when your hunger has been satisfied. Many of us continue to eat long after our hunger pangs have subsided. When you sense that you have eaten enough, stop.

- When everyone has finished and the mindfulness meal is over, the participants might engage in some quiet chatting, perhaps even discussing their experience.

- Like preparation, the clean up can be done in a meditative way, but it may be harder to do so because you usually want it done with as soon as possible. The mindfulness approach is to reorient your attention from getting the job finished to staying aware of what you're doing.

Questions to Consider

1. Reflect on the ways you can integrate mindfulness practices into your everyday eating experiences. What aspects of the rest of your life do you need to change in order to accommodate mindful eating?

2. Invite a like-minded friend, or group of friends, to spend an evening together cooking and enjoying a mindfulness supper using the principles suggested in this lecture.

Driving—Staying Awake at the Wheel
Lecture 12

A s you drive mindfully, you will notice that you have little control over the full range of events that are unfolding before your eyes. You have slight, if any, authority over what others do. Your powers are fairly limited to the control you have over your own vehicle, but even that is not absolute. Despite your limitations, it is possible to sit back, relax, and become mindfully alert to your experiences. You'll see interesting things, scary things, things that will make you sad, things that will make you laugh—but you'll always keep going.

Driving in the United States

- Operating motor vehicles is an extremely important part of American culture. According to the Bureau of Transportation, there are more automobiles in the United States than licensed drivers. In the first decade of the 21st century, Americans drove approximately 3 trillion miles each year.

- Because we spend so much time on the road, driving represents a wonderful opportunity for us to practice mindfulness. Like walking and eating, driving is an ordinary experience whose potential for enriching our awareness of life is usually overlooked.

- Practicing mindfulness while driving is not only a choice opportunity; it's also a veritable necessity. Driving may be the most hazardous activity the average person participates in. Each year, there are well over 6 million vehicle collisions in the United States, in which 3 million people suffer injuries.

- Certainly, a major factor in many accidents is the lack of attentiveness, whether that's caused by cell phone use, eating food, engaging in conversations, or just driving under the influence of mindlessness. If there's anything we do that can benefit from the application of mindfulness, it's operating a vehicle.

- Are you a mindless driver? Take a moment to assess your ordinary driving habits. Consider how often you fail to drive completely attentive to the experience as it's happening. It's not uncommon for people to drive for miles and miles without paying full attention to the route they're taking.

- Think also about the way you drive. Do you drive aggressively? Timidly? Competitively? Do you drive lawfully, always observing speed limits and other traffic regulations? Many people don't always feel obligated to obey the rules when they're on the road. If you think of your automobile as an extension of your personality, as some psychologists suggest it is, what does your driving say about you?

Each year, about 40,000 people die in vehicle mishaps. Therefore, driving mindfully is a necessity.

Driving Mindfully

- Mindful driving begins long before you enter the car. Because driving is a potentially hazardous activity, we should do all we can beforehand to ensure our journeys are safe.

- First, that means making sure the vehicle we're driving is well maintained and in good operating condition. Second, it means preparing our minds to take the responsibility of driving seriously, knowing that getting behind the wheel requires our full attention. If we're unprepared for that responsibility, we should at least be responsible enough not to drive.

- When you're ready to go, bring mindful attention to what you're doing as you approach the car. You might start by engaging in a walking meditation practice as you move toward your vehicle; then, stay attentive as you go through the usual routine of preparing to drive, such as buckling up and fixing your mirrors.

- If you have passengers, make sure everyone is prepared and safely buckled. Remember that the safety of yourself, the others in the car, and strangers on the road depends on your full awareness. Careful driving is an act of compassion. Therefore, you should focus on the experience of driving and not on the destination.

- As you prepare to leave, reflect on the value of removing potential distractions, just as you would for sitting meditation. Try driving without the radio, coffee, or any other possible distractions and study the effect of its absence on your attentiveness.

- Then, check your posture. Make sure you're sitting in a position that promotes alertness and allows you to be relaxed. Keep your hands firmly on the steering wheel, but don't clench them. They, too, should feel relaxed. Perhaps you can manage a quick body scan to release any tension you may feel. Take several deep breaths and go.

- As you begin to drive, do so normally. There is no need to slow your rate of speed as we do in walking and eating meditation. On the other hand, you might experiment with driving a bit slower than usual to see if that affects your ability to stay attentive. Slightly breaking the routine can help keep your mind focused.

Driving with Anchors

- As we do in other forms of meditation, we'll need to establish anchors as a way to stabilize our attention when it begins to wander. In driving practice, we'll use two.

- The first is the visual field available to us as we look through the car windshield and windows. You'll be paying attention to all items that come within your field of vision—other cars, pedestrians, signs and stoplights, buildings, and so on.

- Most of the time, you will anchor your attention on the visual field in general rather than on anything in particular. Occasionally, of course, it will become necessary to focus on specific things in your view as they become relevant to your driving.

- The second anchor in mindful driving is the sensation of the hands on the steering wheel. It's a good practice, both for mindfulness and for safety's sake, to keep both hands on the wheel. If you're in the habit of driving with one hand, it will take a good bit of mindfulness just to remember to use both hands.

- In mindful driving, the hands function like the feet in walking meditation. Just as you do with the feet in walking, bring your awareness to the sensations of the hands. You may feel the hardness or softness of the wheel itself, some pain or tension in your hands, or the vibrations generated by the engine and the car as it moves.

- The basic practice of driving mindfully is quite simple. It follows the observe-and-return dynamic of sitting meditation. Whenever you notice your mind drifting away from being attentive to the experience of driving, gently escort your awareness back to these two anchors, which ground you in the present.

- In driving, it's possible to create specific ways to remind yourself to return to the present moment. If you're driving in town, you can designate certain recurring markers—such as intersections, traffic lights, or stop signs—as prompters to jog your memory. If you're on the highway, telephone or light poles might serve the same function.

- Wherever you are, use markers to remind you to drop your thoughts and reacquaint yourself with the present moment. Bring your attention back to the visual field and then feel the sensations of your hands and proceed.

- Make a determination to keep your eye on the road. When the next marker appears, note how successful you were at staying attentive, return to your anchors, and continue. Over time, repeating this practice will allow your attention to remain concentrated on driving.

Nonvisual Sensations

- As you begin to master the basic technique, you can start to work with other aspects of your experience. Keeping the mind focused on the visual field and the sensations of the hands affords the occasional opportunity to attend to other aspects of your bodily experience. Every so often, you can take a moment to check your posture and make adjustments if necessary. You can notice if any areas of your body are contracted or tense and allow them to relax.

- A good time to review your bodily experience is whenever you pull up to a red light. You can also concentrate attention on specific physical functions involved in operating the vehicle, such as using your foot to brake or rotating your head to scan your field of vision.

- As you continue with the practice, you can add the sensation of hearing to the experiences you observe. As you drive, you can spend a moment listening to the sound of your engine. This practice not only keeps your attention in the present, but it can also alert you if there is something wrong with your car.

- Driving involves all sorts of other interesting sounds when you take time to listen: the humming of the tires on the road, the whir of the air conditioning or heater, and the clamorous noises of traffic. As with sitting meditation, try to stay attentive to the sensations themselves; if you find yourself drifting off into thought about the sensations, gently escort attention back to your anchors.

- Once you've become comfortable returning awareness to your field of vision and observing your bodily sensations, you can begin to give systematic attention to your emotions. Being aware of the emotional aspect of your experience is extremely important in driving practice because emotions play an extremely important role in driving.

- Out on the road, we're apt to have many occasions to feel anger, frustration, fear, and surprise. Think of how often you've found yourself getting angry at other motorists or at traffic delays. Driving can be an emotionally charged experience, and it can certainly take its toll on our general sense of well-being.

- As in other forms of meditation, our aim in driving practice is to observe these emotions arising without judgment and allowing them to fall away, preserving our equanimity. You don't have to act on these emotions, just witness them. Of course, it takes a great deal of practice to permit such powerful emotions as anger and fear to arise and fall without reacting in a negative way.

- Almost everyone feels irritation, if not outright rage, when we come upon some kind of traffic delay, even if it's relatively brief. The mindfulness approach is to acknowledge the situation and recognize our limited powers to change it. You can welcome these moments as an opportunity to think about things you haven't had the time to contemplate—permitting your reflections to run as deep as you like.

- Even as you allow these ruminations in stalled traffic, you should frequently return to the visual field and maintain touch with your present situation. It's certainly fine to ponder the future and recall the past, but always do so with the awareness of what you're doing.

- Of course, driving isn't just about dealing with maniacs, idiots, and traffic jams. It can also be about having pleasurable experiences. It's a fascinating world out there, and driving is one way to see it. However, in order to see it, you have to be awake. You have to marshal your capacities for attention and train your mind to see what is occurring in each moment.

Driving as a Metaphor

- Driving, in fact, is a kind of metaphor for the journey through life. You're moving through the world on pathways generally established by others who've come before you. Occasionally, you may go off the beaten path and discover something very interesting or something very terrifying. You may stop for a while, but eventually you'll keep going.

- As you're traveling along, you may have a general idea about what's up ahead, but you can never be certain. There are always surprises and possible dangers, even along your habitual routes. There are delays and detours, smooth pavement and potholes, nice people and not-so-nice people. You can unwittingly take a wrong turn and travel down a road that will change your life forever—or you can stick to the main road and never deviate from it.

Questions to Consider

1. How does ordinary driving affect you? How does it influence your emotions and your ability to pay attention? What past experiences have shaped your experience of driving? How does driving reflect the rest of your life?

2. Schedule 30 minutes to devote yourself to driving mindfully. Don't plan a destination. Simply have the single purpose to drive in complete awareness for that amount of time.

Insight—Clearing the Mind

Lecture 13

Insight into transience is central to mindfulness practice. How we respond to the fact of impermanence determines whether we suffer or find lasting happiness in the world. The mindfulness tradition tells us that change is nothing to fear and that it is possible to live a life of contentment amid a world of constant flux. However, to overcome our fear of change and to find equanimity in its midst requires clearly gazing into it. It is here that words must stop, and we must return to the silence of meditation.

The Element of Insight

- We've all had moments when things suddenly become clear. The haze dissipates, and what was there all along becomes obvious. The solution to the problem you've been pondering unexpectedly presents itself. The issue you've been struggling with dissolves, your heart catches fire with inspiration, and immediately you know what you must do. Sometimes we wonder how we could have missed what is now so plainly apparent.

- Mindfulness practice promises these unmistakable moments when something within you moves and you see things differently. Appropriately enough, the mindfulness tradition calls these moments "insights," or "clear gazing," to translate the Buddhist word *vipassana*.

- The element of insight distinguishes mindfulness practice from forms of meditation that seek only to calm the mind. In mindfulness, stilling the mind is essential, but it is only a precondition for a deeper purpose: to gain insight into the way the world is and to live our lives accordingly. We cannot coerce insights, but we can use meditation to clear the way for them to arise.

- If you have been continuing with a daily mindfulness practice, you have already been doing the necessary groundwork for insight. In fact, you may have already experienced insights and started to feel that a whole new world is opening up to you.

- Meditation helps us to be more attentive to our lives. At the same time, it enables us to develop a new relationship with our experience, characterized by acceptance and relinquishment. The qualities of attention, acceptance, and relinquishment are what prime our minds for insight.

- We learn through meditation that just because a thought arises does not mean we have to believe it. If we simply accept the fact that it has arisen and let it go, without aversion or attachment, the mind remains clear, spacious, and ready to see what is there.

- When a mind is so full of thoughts and ideas about the way things are and the way things should be, it lacks the flexibility and openness to see the world in a new way. The problem with such a mind is not that it has ideas and opinions; the difficulty is the way it clings to these thoughts with such tenacity.

- Meditation practice enables us to recognize our ideas and beliefs, accept them for what they are, and remain unattached to them. We allow our thoughts and sensations to arise and then allow them to go their own way.

The Beginner's Mind

- It requires constant practice to prevent ourselves from becoming experts. Staying a beginner means having to start over and over again. One way to stay a beginner—or become one—is to practice **not-knowing**, which begins with an honest assessment of what we really know and what we really can know.

- Most of what we as individuals profess as "knowledge" is perhaps better categorized as "belief." Everyone "knows" the world is a sphere, but how many of us have actually taken the trouble to verify that for ourselves? Consider how much of what we think we know has been received on the basis of this sort of faith.

- It is impossible as well as unnecessary to take the time to verify everything we claim to know, but recognizing that so much of what we call knowledge is founded on implicit trust in authorities rather than on immediate personal experience ought at least to make us cautious about asserting anything with too much conviction.

- Most of us feel great pressure to be knowledgeable—or at least appear that way. We learn early in our careers how to speak with the authority to convince others and ourselves that we know what we're talking about. Sometimes, of course, we do know what we're talking about.

- The truth is that we really know less than we think, and much of what we profess to know is actually belief, opinion, and conjecture. This is especially true when it comes to facing the great questions in life: From whence have we come and why? Does life have a meaning or purpose? What happens when we die?

- Knowledge—or even just the illusion of knowledge—provides us with a hedge against the terrors of uncertainty. It furnishes us with the pleasant feeling that we are actually in control of our lives.

- To practice not-knowing means finding the courage to be at ease with uncertainty and mystery. Essentially, one overcomes the fear of the unknown by becoming more familiar with it. Certainly, meditation helps us with this.

- In our practice, all manner of thoughts and feelings arise, and we are encouraged simply to be with them. Rather than making us feel secure by answering all our questions, mindfulness practice invites us to become free from attachment to security, free from the frantic need to know, and free from the ego's desire to appear knowledgeable.

- The Buddha was renowned for refusing to answer questions. Unlike many other sages of his era, and even sages of our era, the Buddha did not feel compelled to provide a comprehensive worldview that could explain any question that might arise in the mind.

- Not-knowing does not mean one necessarily lacks knowledge or that we're required to forget everything or to suspend all interpretations of a situation. Not-knowing does not mean that we are confused. Rather, it is a consciously chosen attitude that we take to allow us to see things more clearly. It is the acknowledgement that we may not understand everything we need to know to handle a particular situation.

- Maintaining a beginner's mind, practicing not-knowing, relaxing attachments to thoughts, being humble, learning to live with uncertainty—these are all interrelated aspects of clearing the way for insight. Insight comes when our minds are ready. This must be why moments of crisis are often times of great spiritual development.

- Such cognitively disorienting occasions as death, divorce, and addiction carry the potential to disrupt old habits of mind and to open us to new ways of seeing. These are often times when uncertainty, not-knowing, and humility are thrust upon us. If we are wise and attentive, these critical times can be gifts of great value.

For Zen Buddhists, seeking to understand the true nature of Zen is the same as wanting to know the true nature of reality.

- When we speak of insight in the mindfulness tradition, we are speaking of something more than just discovering a solution to a problem—although a mindful insight may lead to that. We're speaking of something more than just a profound thought that suddenly occurs to us—although insight may coalesce into profound thinking.

- Insight in mindfulness is understood as an immediate experience of clarity about the nature of reality. There is nothing supernatural about insight. It is the ordinary, natural experience of seeing the world as it is, devoid of the heavy overlay of preconceptions and beliefs that clutter our perceptions of it.

- Insight pertains more to the function of perception than to thinking. Thinking, of course, precedes insight and may proceed from it, but insight itself is distinguishable from thinking. The very same sense is conveyed by the original meaning of the English word "insight," which is "to see into."

Three Principal Insights: Transience

- While there are an infinite number of possible insights into human existence, Buddhism focuses on three that pertain to the heart of our experience of reality. These are known as the three marks, or characteristics, of existence.

- The three insights are transience, or impermanence; not-self, or the "illusion and insubstantiality of the self"; and dukkha, a word that is usually translated as "suffering" but whose meaning is rich and deep.

- Insight into these three qualities is regarded by Buddhists as essential to freedom and happiness. In addition, Buddhism argues that these qualities of our experience are interrelated and so to gain insight into one is to also see the other two.

- When the tradition insists that these three characteristics must be grasped by insight, we must bear in mind that these are not regarded as beliefs to which one gives assent, nor are they simply concepts to be grasped by the intellect. They are considered facts about the nature of existence that must be apprehended by direct personal experience.

- Transience, or impermanence, is the name for the insight that is probably the easiest to understand. Everyone acknowledges that things change, but the mindfulness tradition contends that most of us fail to acknowledge the depth of change without qualification, and hence we live resisting the impermanence over which we have no control.

- When it comes to the reality of change, we often look for ways to believe we are somehow exempt from it. Perhaps the chasm between what we believe to be true and how we live our lives can be explained by a lack of genuine insight.

- We grasp the idea of impermanence conceptually, but impermanence has not yet grasped us in the way that insight makes possible—in the manner that revolutionizes our whole way of life.

- Meditative practice makes it possible to sharpen perceptive attention to such a degree that one can have a direct knowledge of the momentary arising and passing away of all reality. When viewed this way, any perception of stability or permanence is only apparent.

- A deep, penetrating awareness of the world reveals that all things are concatenations of events happening so rapidly that they seem to be stable or changing only very slowly.

- If you have a chance, spend a few moments outside and contemplate an ordinary tree—or simply imagine one. To the casual observer, a tree appears to be a more or less stable thing, but looking deeper, we can see it is a grand spectacle of ever-changing processes happening in swift succession at every level of its existence. From this perspective, a tree is not—and cannot be—the same from moment to moment.

- Change is so far-reaching, so thoroughgoing, that ultimately we can say there are no "things" in the world at all. No item in our experience—no thought, feeling, or physical object—endures long enough from one moment to the next for us to say it is a "thing," an entity that has its own existence in space and time.

- Our minds, conditioned as they are by our language, tend to reify, or regard as concrete things, matters that are better understood as events or occurrences. The danger arises only when we forget that talking and thinking about "things" is a mere convenient contrivance. The true reality of the world of existence is something that cannot be easily captured by our thought and language—but it can be grasped by insight.

Important Terms

not-knowing: A beginning practice that starts with an honest assessment of what one really knows and what one really can know.

vipassana: The Buddhist word for "insights" or "clear gazing," these are unmistakable moments when a person sees things differently.

Questions to Consider

1. Choose a simple object, like a vase or chair, to look at. Take a moment to become mindful of your breathing. Then, place your attention on the object. Try to observe the object as clearly and as naïvely as possible without the usual overlay of conceptual thought. How does this approach differ from your usual manner of observation?

2. Reflect on how much of what you think you know is based on belief and faith and how much is founded on personal experience.

Wisdom—Seeing the World as It Is
Lecture 14

Transience, dukkha, and not-self are interrelated marks of existence. The failure to apprehend that people are subject to impermanence and insubstantiality gives rise to dukkha, and the experience of dukkha reinforces our misapprehensions. By imputing permanent selfhood where there is none, we effectively believe ourselves to be individual entities whose fragile existences must be propped up by possessions, achievements, beliefs, and relationships—but that is an illusion. Paradoxically, when we awaken to reality, we discover that the only way to find happiness is to relinquish these feverish efforts to protect and empower the mistaken belief we call the self.

The Quest for Happiness

- Like Aristotle, Mencius, and a great many other thinkers, the Buddha thought that the quest for lasting happiness was the principal impulse of human activity. Aristotle said happiness was the one thing we seek for itself and not as a means to something else; whether we're aware of it or not, happiness is the true aim of all we do. The Buddha would have agreed.

- Neither the Buddha nor Aristotle, however, conceived of happiness in the way we're apt to think of it these days—as a pleasurable experience. The Buddha understood happiness as an enduring reality that is not contingent on fleeting pleasures. This kind of contentment is what all beings truly want and seek.

- While he regarded the desire for happiness to be natural and wholesome, the Buddha did see serious problems with the ways we try to satisfy that yearning. Because we lack wisdom, because we fail to see the world as it is, we inevitably go about the pursuit of happiness in the very ways that sabotage its fulfillment.

- Without awakening to the true nature of reality—without insight into the three marks of existence—we seek contentment in the wrong places and through the wrong means. Because we can never find it, our thirst for satisfaction intensifies and worsens.

Acquisition

- Most of us seek happiness in two basic ways: the first is by acquisition, which is the preferred method in the modern world, and the second is by aversion, which is trying to avoid unpleasant situations. Both techniques are based on what Sigmund Freud called the **pleasure principle**—grasping for the things that we enjoy and evading the things we don't.

- The quest for contentment through acquisition usually leads us to try to enhance our lives by surrounding ourselves with things we believe will give us pleasure: homes, cars, clothing, trophies, and other commonly accepted markers of well-being and achievement.

- Acquisitiveness, however, need not focus on material items. One can seek happiness by having unique and interesting experiences—including spiritual experiences—or by holding the right religious or political beliefs or by affiliating with an organization or a cause.

- If we fail to get what we want, of course, we usually suffer. Because we have made the acquisition of a particular thing the condition for our contentment, not getting it leaves us feeling sad, disappointed, frustrated, and perhaps angry—thinking we've missed the very thing that would have made us happy.

Life's Two Tragedies

- A lot of our remembrance of the past is a reflection on the times we didn't get what we wanted—the first tragedy of life. Tragedy two appears when we actually get what we want.

- Getting what we want may indeed bring us great pleasure, but the pleasurable feelings won't last. When the initial pleasure subsides, disappointment sets in. Disappointment comes in exact proportion to how much happiness we expected our acquisition to provide.

- Desires, whether they are fulfilled or frustrated, only beget more desires. There is no end to our desires when we think that fulfilling our wishes is the way to happiness.

Aversion

Getting what we want may indeed bring us great pleasure, but the pleasurable feelings won't last.

- Alongside acquisition, we also seek satisfaction by avoiding unpleasant situations, things, or people. Aversion is actually just the opposite of acquisition; both are manifestations of desire. As with acquisition, the problem with trying to find your happiness through avoidance is the nature of reality. Reality simply does not allow us to evade unwanted experiences.

- We might be able to escape a few unwanted experiences, but the evasive life often comes at a cost. Even if we can successfully ward off some terrifying experiences, we cannot avert them all—particularly the most unpleasant ones: sickness, old age, and death.

Three Principal Insights: Dukkha

- If our strategy has been to flee from unpleasant circumstances, when they come to meet us, as they surely will, our suffering will be great indeed. These difficult situations are all encompassed by the Buddhist word **dukkha**, which denotes the fundamental frustrating, insatiable quality of our mindless existence.

- Usually translated into English as suffering or dissatisfaction, the meaning of dukkha is actually far richer than a single English word, or even a cluster of English words, can express. You might find it translated as illness, anguish, sorrow, unease, distress, unsettledness, lamentation, pain, grief, despair, and disappointment.

- Dukkha does not merely characterize episodes or aspects of existence. It does not simply suggest that life has a lot of sorrow and anguish, although it does mean that. Rather, the term dukkha indicates that sorrow and anguish, suffering and disappointment permeate existence.

- Dukkha is pervasive, subtle, and insidious—not merely episodic. Like impermanence, there are no exceptions to dukkha in the conditioned world of life as we ordinarily know it. Dukkha names every aspect of experience in which there is the slightest twinge or possibility of anxiety, fear, or disappointment.

- In its full sense, dukkha is not a readily apparent fact of life but a challenge for individuals to discover for themselves by means of introspection and observation. As with the facts of transience, the surface of dukkha can be grasped conceptually, but its depth can only be seen by insight.

An Exercise in Dukkha

- Schedule an appointment with disappointment. Determine to spend an entire day trying to be mindful of all your disappointments and frustrations—no matter how small. If you find this approach too demanding, take some time at the end of a day for reflection.

- As you prepare for the day or reflect back on it, consider the potential sources of routine disappointment: When you're on the road, how's the traffic? Does anyone say something to hurt your feelings? After you've tallied up your disappointing experiences, reflect on how you reacted to them.

- With continued observation and mindfulness practice, the reality of dukkha becomes clearer, and we begin to gain insight into its source and its cure. Eventually, we realize that dukkha is the result of one thing: the fact that the world does not always conform to our desires and expectations.

- The world's not to blame, of course. Reality just is what it is. The problem is with our desires and expectations. We simply expect too much from the world.

- Insight lets us see that the whole approach to contentment through acquisition or aversion is fundamentally misguided. Rather than bringing the satisfaction we so deeply want, acquisition and aversion only serve to frustrate us and increase our anguish and disappointment.

- Instead of questioning these methods themselves, we foolishly think in our mindless state that we simply haven't acquired or averted the right thing or enough things.

Three Principal Insights: Not-Self

- The third mark of existence—and the most difficult to grasp both by intellect and by insight—is **not-self**, which is sometimes compared to "insubstantiality." Not-self is even difficult for those within the tradition to understand, yet it is central to the Buddhist worldview.

- By observing the radical depth of transience, we have already begun to make our acquaintance with the mark of not-self. Insight into impermanence reveals that nothing maintains sameness or identity over successive moments or exists independently of other realities.

- Consequently, the idea of a thing, an entity enduring through time and having its own separate existence, is potentially a misleading habit of the mind. Ultimately, there is no such thing as a thing.

- This idea sounds fine as long as we're considering trees and other items in the world, but when it comes to the human person, we become a bit more apprehensive.

- As we observed in the previous lecture, people want to exempt themselves somehow from the reality of impermanence, even against evidence to the contrary. One of the ways we try to make an exception for ourselves is through the concept of the soul or a permanent self.

- Almost every religious and many philosophical worldviews posit an immortal soul or some version of an unchanging self in which the personality has a core identity that endures even if the body dies.

- Even some modern views in psychology maintain the existence of a "true self" that underlies so many false selves or masks of our personality.

- Not-self is nothing more than a denial of the idea of an immortal soul or an enduring self. It simply means that human beings are not exempt from the quality of impermanence; our every aspect is subject to change.

- Not-self does not mean that human beings do not really exist or are unreal. We exist and are real, but we do not exist in the way we're accustomed to think. Problems arise when we reify the concept of the self—when we begin to think of the self as a real thing.

- If we take the concept of self as referring to something real and permanent, we mobilize the rest of our lives to accommodate it. On the basis of a self, we create all manner of self-centered desires, and on the basis of those desires, we and others suffer. That is dukkha.

- In view of the tendency of the idea of the self to cause damage, the mindfulness tradition, as well as other religious and philosophical traditions throughout the world, maintains that it is in our best interest—and in the best interest of everyone—to relinquish our attachment to self and to live without putting ourselves at the hub of the universe.

- No matter how wholesome it may be, relinquishing the idea of self may be the most difficult thing a person can do. We are so attached to this sense of self that we believe giving it up will mean our demise. However, many thinkers and traditions throughout history have suggested that this is precisely the way to lasting happiness.

- What we must realize, according to the Buddhist mindfulness tradition, is that all we are letting go of is a fiction, a fabrication of the mind that causes us to suffer. It is not our true identity; it is not who we really are.

- We should also realize that letting go of the self, or ego if you prefer, does not mean we are on a crusade to destroy it. If we simply refrain from acting as if it were real, the self—a thought like any other—will fall away of its own accord. Paradoxically, if we try to annihilate the self, we will only empower it.

An Exercise in Not-Self

- During a sitting meditation practice, spend some time reflecting on these questions. When I refer to myself, what exactly do I mean? When I use the word "I," to what does that refer? Is there anything about me that endures or is permanent? If so, what is it? How do I know it's there? Is there anything about me that does not rely on something else for its existence?

dukkha: A Buddhist term that basically means "suffering" and that denotes the fundamental frustrating, insatiable quality of the mindless existence of human beings.

not-self: A term that is sometimes compared to "insubstantiality." This is the third mark of existence that is central to the Buddhist worldview—and the most difficult to grasp both by intellect and by insight, even for those within the tradition.

pleasure principle: A term introduced by Sigmund Freud that describes the way in which people grasp for the things they enjoy and evade the things they don't.

Questions to Consider

1. Why is getting what we want so often unable to provide us with satisfaction?

2. Do you agree that belief in a permanent, substantial self leads to the experience of what the Buddha called dukkha?

Compassion—Expressing Fundamental Kindness
Lecture 15

S ome of the noblest aspirations of the human heart include the ability to see wrong and try to right it, to see suffering and try to heal it, and to see war and try to stop it. These phrases also offer a precise description of the essence of compassion. For most of us, the skill to be compassionate toward difficult people comes at the end of a very long road. Mindfulness can guide you through working with the easier cases and help you gradually progress to the harder ones.

Compassion versus Pity

- **Compassion** is the desire to alleviate suffering—or dukkha, to use the richer term. Compassion entails the courage to face dukkha, the wisdom to gaze into it deeply, and the resolve to respond to it in a way that brings relief.

- More than just a sentiment, compassion is born of a brave consciousness and a strong will. It may arise as tenderness in the heart, but it requires the support of a tough mind.

- Compassion is not pity, although the two are sometimes confused. **Pity** is simply feeling sorry for someone who has to endure suffering, but pity keeps its distance from suffering. Pity can't get past the element of fear; it's afraid of pain and suffering and wants to flee from their presence.

- Compassion doesn't keep its distance; it literally means "to experience or endure with." Compassion is willing to be with suffering up close because it has learned to accept rather than resist suffering.

- Words are sometimes used to hide our discomfort with suffering. Sometimes we just don't know what to say, but it's better to keep quiet than to utter vacuous words. The compassionate person does not flee from pain or silence.

- Even without words, one can bring comfort to another by merely being physically present and mindfully attentive. Such gestures can strengthen others by conveying that it is possible neither to resist nor run away from suffering.

- The capacity for compassion is in our deepest nature as human beings. To be sure, some of us manifest the face of compassion more plainly than others. Many consider motherhood to be the prime exemplar of compassion.

- In the Tanakh—the Hebrew Bible—the word translated as compassion derives from the same root syllable from which the word for womb comes. In fact, the word for womb, *rehem*, is itself occasionally translated as compassion. Both words are related etymologically to *ar-Rahman*, meaning "the exceedingly compassionate," one of the Qur'an's 99 most beautiful names for God.

- When we fail to act in a compassionate way, as we often do, we have either been conditioned to ignore suffering, or we have suppressed the desire to relieve it. Our frequent failure to be compassionate does not mean that compassion is not a basic part of who we are; it simply means that our fundamental nature has been obscured and needs to be gently revealed.

- Much in our modern culture works to separate us from our basic compassion and, hence, alienate us from one another and from ourselves. Our love of competition, our fear of pain and suffering, our quest for pleasure, and our endless forms of distraction all function to enshroud compassion.

- As we continue with daily sitting practice, occasional body scans, walking meditation, and mindful eating, we subtly counteract those deadening aspects of our culture. Whether we recognize it or not, mindfulness practice quietly subverts those forces and gently eases their effects on us.

The Cultivation of Compassion

- Being able to see dukkha is the prerequisite to deeper compassion, but perceiving the deeper expressions of suffering isn't easy and requires the skills of attentiveness that mindfulness practice sharpens.

- Seeing the extensive and subtle nature of dukkha permits us to be more adept at identifying it and becoming more familiar with it. That familiarity, in turn, helps us to accept it as present-moment experience, which we need not run from or resist.

- Compassion requires the willingness to look at suffering, tragedy, and pain without aversion or attachment. Recognizing the subtle nature of dukkha also enables us to see how its clearly evident manifestations, such as war and conflict, are interrelated with its less-apparent forms, such as greed, fear, and disappointment.

- Common to all experiences of dukkha are self-centered desires that often outstrip the capacity of reality to satisfy them. Insight into the conditions that give rise to suffering is necessary to being able to respond to that suffering constructively.

- Recognizing dukkha in our own experience is critical to seeing it in the lives of others. Unless you understand the nature of your own suffering, you can do little to help others with theirs.

- Paradoxically, then, you can take your conditioned tendency to focus on you and use it to turn outward toward others in compassion. As we go further into our practice, however, we begin to see that this is hardly a paradox at all, as we come to understand that there is not your suffering and the suffering of others—there is only suffering.

Compassion and Empathy

- Being compassionate toward others is based on empathy, or what the Buddha called "putting yourself in the place of others." Knowing that you want to be happy and free from suffering, you can infer that other beings want this as well, and you can treat them accordingly.

- The first step in being compassionate toward others thus involves imaginatively entering into the interiority of another person, sharing his or her inner life in a profound way by recognizing that they are like you.

- The world's religions and philosophies almost uniformly endorse this empathetic precept and make it the cornerstone of their ethics. It is the basis of what we in the West call the Golden Rule: "Do unto others as you would have them do unto you."

- In East Asia, many follow the same principle as it was formulated by Confucius over 2,500 years ago: "Never impose on others what you would not choose for yourself." If you do a little research, you might be surprised by how widely and frequently this simple idea is articulated in the world's wisdom traditions.

- Despite its ubiquity, most of us find it difficult to remember to be empathetic, which may be a clue as to why the principle is so repeatedly articulated in the traditions.

- It's not that empathy is particularly difficult for us. Sometimes, it arises within us spontaneously, perhaps more than we ordinarily recognize—unless we're paying attention. Just as often, however, we neglect to practice empathy because the illusion of self gets in the way.

- Your conditioned tendency to regard the universe as revolving around you makes it easy to forget that the rest of the world thinks the universe revolves around them. When you're so absorbed in seeking your own happiness by means of the usual frantic and misguided methods, you're too preoccupied to appreciate that others are seeking the same freedom from suffering that you are.

- If we can just look around—at our world and at each other—taking some time to stop the futile climbing up and sliding down, we can see what a state we're really in. That awareness changes our whole attitude toward the world and toward each other.

Empathy in Practice

- When you're not feeling particularly empathetic with some of your fellow human beings, there is a simple practice to remind you of the common humanity we all share beneath the labels and identifications that divide us. Any time you discover yourself being annoyed by or feeling alienated from someone, recite the words "just like me."

- If you're seeking an ideal location for testing your progress on the mindfulness path, there's no better place than an airport. Where else do you have such wonderful opportunities to experience the subtle manifestations of dukkha, to practice patience and anger management, to observe other people, and even to meditate?

- Let's say you find yourself waiting in one of the several airport queues you have to go through to get to where you're going. Just ahead of you as you're rushing to get through security is a bumbling passenger who has no clue how to negotiate this procedure expeditiously.

- As you watch the bumbling passenger, it is the perfect time to practice your skills of empathy. Say to yourself: "Just like me. Here is a person who forgot to empty his pockets: It's so easy to get flustered going through these stressful queues that I can understand how someone could overlook that step."

- You don't know what is ailing the pushy woman behind you or the slow man in front of you in line. What you do know is they are seeking happiness just like you—and probably doing so in the same misguided ways as you.

- "Just like me" is a versatile practice. It can be performed just about anywhere, at any time. You can practice as you read about or watch events in the news, taking a moment to ponder why others behave the way they do, trying to imagine how you would react in a similar situation, reflecting on the ways we share a common humanity.

- "Just like me" is extremely effective for establishing empathy with others, particularly those we find difficult to like. Empathy and compassion do not require that we feel affection for the other. We can have compassion for our worst enemies.

- Ultimately, the full pursuit of compassion practice requires that we cultivate empathy for some very tough characters, including those whom we know to be the perpetrators of horrendous violence and abuse. Compassion cannot be selective.

- There is one very tough character you'll have to work with before you can go any further with this practice: yourself. For some of us, it may be harder to muster compassion for ourselves than for others.

- There is a saying attributed to the Buddha: "You can search throughout the entire universe for someone who is more deserving of your love and compassion than you are yourself, and that person is not to be found anywhere. You yourself, as much as anybody, deserve your love and compassion."

Important Terms

compassion: The desire to alleviate suffering.

pity: Feeling sorry for someone who has to endure suffering.

1. Recall a time when you were the recipient of another's compassion. What effects did that experience have on your state of mind?

2. Do you accept the idea that compassion is an inherent part of who we are? Why or why not? Either way, compassion needs cultivation.

Imperfection—Embracing Our Flaws
Lecture 16

The effects of perfectionism are everywhere. We observe perfectionism in the way we readily heap blame and criticism on ourselves, even for the most minor mistakes. We see it in the ways we treat our bodies, condemning them for being too thin or too fat or too old. We notice it in the way we make excessive demands of ourselves, expecting to be wildly successful in our careers or to be model friends or ideal parents. We must come to accept our imperfections—and our inner critic—in order to better understand the world and others.

Checklist for Perfectionism

- Most human beings are afflicted with at least a touch of perfectionism—or perhaps with more than just a touch. If any or all of the following descriptions apply to you, you may be a perfectionist.

    o When you make a mistake, you find it hard to forget. You think about it over and over again—until you make another mistake to take its place or until you get praised for something.

    o Any error—or perceived error—that you make is completely your fault. You think that if you had only been more attentive or thought things out more thoroughly, the misstep wouldn't have occurred.

    o You're constantly comparing yourself with others and you feel painfully vulnerable and totally defeated when you think you've come up short against someone else.

- You're always telling yourself you must try harder. You believe that if can't do something flawlessly, you shouldn't do it at all.

- If you make a mistake in front of others, you think you'll die of embarrassment.

- You're extremely reluctant to ask for help, believing that to do so is to reveal your weakness as person.

- You do everything you can to keep others from seeing this weaker side, and what's worse is that you try to hide this side from yourself, making it extremely difficult to admit your mistakes.

Perfectionist Mindsets

- Perfectionism is the practice of trying to live up to impossible ideals and then feeling worthless when we don't. It's a textbook recipe for dukkha. Perfectionism is not the same as the mere desire to do well by striving to meet high standards.

- Unlike the simple aspiration to excel at what one does, perfectionism involves an insidious attachment to an unrealistic view of the self. Perfectionists believe they can be perfect and must be perfect, and if they can't, they consider themselves utter failures.

- In response to that judgment, perfectionists may become extremely self-critical and attempt virtually anything to rid themselves of the negative feelings those thoughts precipitate.

- One response might be self-punishment, which could be anything from constantly berating oneself to inflicting physical harm. Another might be to turn to intoxicating substances or overeating to silence those voices of derision. Still another is to submit to a grueling regimen in order to make oneself the ideal person one thinks one must be.

- This affliction is one of the major reasons we find it difficult to extend compassion to ourselves. Because we often hold ourselves to unrealistic standards, we sometimes find it hard to believe that we actually deserve compassion.

- What lies beneath resistance to self-compassion is a completely egocentric belief that, even though perfection is out of reach for most mortals, you are different—you are not like the ordinary person. Some religious traditions attribute this overweening attitude to a desire to be like God.

Perfectionism and Spirituality

- Over 1,600 years ago, Saint Augustine observed that the self longed to experience the pleasure of having godlike powers and assuming God's place at the center of the universe. Augustine suggested that this endeavor to be God was precisely what alienated us from the divine, other people, and ourselves; in other words, it was the very thing that caused us to suffer.

- Aspiring to live up to the image of a wholly self-sufficient and perfect being that is beyond reproach can drive us to great misery. Like other forms of suffering, perfectionism stems from an unrealistic view of the self, and it is perhaps the principal obstruction to our practice of self-compassion.

- Developing one's spirituality can hold out the promise of relief for the perfectionist, but at the same time, it can add fuel to the flames when the path becomes another form of achievement.

- Spiritual discipline can provide a means for sinners to receive punishment and a way for the saints to attain sanctity. Neither of these are goals of the mindfulness path, but that doesn't mean that people won't seek mindfulness as a way to purge themselves of guilt or to reach sainthood.

- To put it in more secular terms, some may seek mindfulness as a method of self-improvement. Mindfulness is for awareness—not expiation, sainthood, or self-improvement.

- On a spiritual pathway, perfectionism can manifest as an obsession with doing everything right. When you learn that perfectionism may hinder your capacity to show compassion to yourself, then you'll most likely eliminate perfectionism.

- Trying to be perfect takes a massive amount of energy, and in the end, it's a futile effort. Therefore, why not just accept the fact that perfection is completely unrealistic and yet you still want to be perfect? Be mindful of both your imperfection and your perfectionism. After all, perfectionism is part of your imperfection.

- You probably see the flaws in human nature everywhere—in other people—and you probably already believe that imperfection is a human quality. The difficulty is in accepting that you're human like everyone else. For some reason, you think you're exceptional.

- In a scriptural story, Siddhattha Gotama—the man who became the Buddha—is depicted as a king's son who is naïve about the fact that sickness, old age, and death apply to him, too. Eventually, he accepts his own participation in the human experience.

- We perfectionists need to come to the same awareness. There are no exemptions from human nature: We'll get sick, we'll get old, we'll die, and we'll make thousands of mistakes along the way.

- If we need help with this insight, the practice of "just like me" can be very effective. When introduced, that exercise was to show how extending empathy to others could rouse compassion for them, but we can also practice the exercise with the reverse goal in mind—to awaken compassion for ourselves.

- Seeing others act in less-than-perfect ways gives us the opportunity to recall to ourselves that we, too, do not always act in an ideal manner. In fact, when something about another person annoys you, let that be a signal to be extremely mindful and look within.

- We usually judge others for the very things we hate about ourselves. Try to turn those judgments of others around and make them an opportunity for extending compassion to yourself.

- Revising our views on perfection may also help. If we understand perfection as the state of being flawless or immaculate, then our striving for these qualities is sure to cause us anguish, but perhaps we can think of perfection in a way that is different from our conditioned way.

Buddhism and Perfectionism

- The Buddhist-influenced aesthetic ideal known in Japan as wabi-sabi seeks to highlight the beautiful aspects of impermanence, incompleteness, and defectiveness. Wabi-sabi values things that are rustic, asymmetrical, irregular, simple, and understated.

- Objects that are worn or in the process of decay are appreciated both for their beauty as well as the spiritual truth they express about the transience and unfinished nature of life. Many of the classical art forms of Japan reflect this aesthetic sensibility—practices such as raku pottery, ikebana flower arranging, and haiku poetry.

- Wabi-sabi invites us to look at life through a lens different from the one offered by perfectionism. The wabi-sabi view of life encourages you to feel more at home in the world, a world where all things, including yourself, could be regarded as aesthetically pleasing just for being what they are—subject to change, incomplete, and less than ideal.

- To help ease your perfectionism, consider surrounding yourself with a few items that embody the wabi-sabi aesthetic to remind yourself that so-called flaws and defects can enhance the beauty of an object. These need not be pieces of art specifically designed as expressions of wabi-sabi. Rather, just take the time to look deliberately for objects that are conventionally flawed and yet bespeak the beauty of the flawed world in which we live.

- In addition, try to embody the wabi-sabi ideal in what you do. Perhaps there is some activity you've wanted to pursue, but you've been hesitant for fear of not being able to do it right. Do it anyway.

- Give up your attachment to success and failure and, instead, focus on the pure joy of what you are doing. If you're a perfectionist, you should find at least one thing in your life about which you can relax your need to succeed.

- We can accept our common lot with humanity and we can try to rethink our understanding of perfection, but the greatest challenge may be embracing our own perfectionism. Trying to eliminate perfectionism is likely to prove counterproductive. There is a massive paradox: Wanting to get rid of perfectionism, if you think about it, is just another form of perfectionism.

- Rather than responding with belligerence to the voice that's constantly criticizing and blaming you, why not try getting to know it better? Let it speak. It will probably do so whether you want to hear it or not.

- Your inner critic is just a voice. You don't have to believe it. You don't have to do what it says. The critical voice of our perfectionism only causes us to suffer when we give it more authority than it deserves.

- Our practice of mindfulness teaches us to allow thoughts to arise and fall on their own—like all impermanent reality. The thought that tells us we must be perfect is just a thought like any other.

- Because trying to silence the critical voice hasn't worked, try to welcome perfectionism as a friend. Treat it with courtesy. Show it some compassion. Appreciate what it's trying to do for you.

- Sometimes, the inner critic says valuable things. It's probably helped you achieve some good things in your life. Sometimes, of course, what the voice of perfectionism tells us is rubbish—but don't most of our friends tell us nonsense from time to time? And we still love them.

Questions to Consider

1. Reflect on your reasons for participating in this course. Are you striving for something? What are you expecting? In what ways may striving for self-improvement thwart the objectives of mindfulness?

2. Consider something that you feel is a flaw in yourself. What will it take for you to come to regard that quality as an asset rather than as a liability?

Wishing—May All Beings Be Well and Happy
Lecture 17

To act, we must call upon our wisdom. Seeing suffering and being willing to heal it does not guarantee that we will act wisely. To be wisely compassionate requires especially that we attend carefully to our own lives and treat ourselves with compassion. What we learn through self-compassion provides important clues for the compassionate treatment of others. Thus, we return to the importance of the Golden Rule. Learning to practice compassion for ourselves and others is a lifetime endeavor, but it is one of the most important things we can do.

The Good and the Bad

- Sometimes it isn't easy to wish others well. Every now and then—perhaps more often than we'd like to admit—we can feel that those who suffer get what they deserve.

- It's especially easy to feel this way about those who have been the source of great suffering to others. We may even take special delight in thinking that those who have caused harm are getting what they deserve.

- However, life is a bit more complicated and less clear cut than we often think it is. It's not always easy to discriminate between good and bad. The differences between all of us are matters of degree rather than quality. There are things we might call "good" and "bad" in each one of us. No one is wholly good, and no one is wholly evil.

- When we see deeply into the life of those we're inclined to despise, we can recognize that whatever vile acts they may commit do not completely express all that they are. We can understand that their hatred and greed arise from fear, self-centeredness, ignorance, and misunderstanding—the very things that afflict all of us from time to time.

- If we ever lose sight of the moral ambiguity that pervades the human condition, we run great risks. Without insight into our own propensity to act in unwholesome ways, we become blind to our own faults. Without insight into the goodness of others, it becomes all too easy to hate them, especially when we feel our hatred is justified by their wrongdoings.

- However, these reactions distort the reality of what we are and lead us to behave unskillfully—in ways that cause suffering to ourselves and others. They incline us to forget how much the personalities of all of us have been shaped by circumstances beyond our control.

- The dangers inherent in forgetting that we're all capable of both wholesome and unwholesome actions have led sages throughout history to urge us to love our enemies, as well as ourselves and our neighbors. This admonition can be considered as one of humanity's truly great moral developments.

- Although loving our enemies may be one of the most difficult things we can possibly do—rivaled perhaps only by loving ourselves—it is clearly one of the most beneficial practices we can perform.

- It's easy to see how hatred lies at the root of much of human misery, but what we seem to find difficult is accepting that we cannot end hatred by hating. Hating those who hate may feel cathartic and even righteous, but it brings us no closer to a solution to what is a very deep problem. Only love and compassion for others can end hostility and hatred; we can never transform an enemy into a friend with hate.

- We also forget what hating others does to us as individuals. Hatred is a manifestation of our false self; it is not what we truly are. To allow ourselves to be consumed by hatred distorts us, wounds us, and scars us.

- Hatred causes us to misperceive the world, confusing the beautiful and the ugly, the true and the false, the skillful and the unskillful.

Hatred is sure to cause us to suffer and is itself a manifestation of suffering.

Alternatives to Hatred

- While it is not difficult to grasp how hatred can perpetuate animosity between people and disfigure our own basic goodness, it is also not easy to find alternatives. How does one erase a lifetime of conditioning in which we have been encouraged to detest others? Hatred can become a habit that is not simple to break.

- Fortunately, the mindfulness tradition offers many practices to help change this pattern, including some we've already discussed. There is one exercise that is particularly effective in awakening the natural compassion that lies within us; this discipline is known as **metta meditation**.

- "Metta" is a Buddhist term that usually translates as "loving-kindness." This ancient practice has long been the cornerstone for cultivating compassion in the Buddhist tradition. It is a great tool for helping us to wish others well and arouse our resolve to alleviate pain and suffering.

- Like other mindfulness techniques, metta meditation requires commitment, regular practice, and patience. It works by reconditioning our mind and opening our hearts. The intention of this practice is to awaken our determination to ease suffering wherever we may find it.

- Metta practice does not discriminate between those who deserve our compassion and those who do not. Compassion is something all beings deserve, even those responsible for horrendous crimes against humanity.

- Metta meditation is a series of wishes for the happiness of all beings. It begins with the recitation of aspirations for oneself and

loved ones and concludes with the same aspirations for all beings—
without exception.

Metta Meditation in Practice

- This guided meditation is a form of the practice that has been
  developed and personalized over the years. Feel free to work with
  this practice and adapt it in ways most suitable to you. For example,
  alter the wording of the aspirations or change the people for whom
  they are intended.

- At the mention of each category, try to picture a particular person
  and keep him or her in your imagination; the practice is more
  effective when we're thinking of particular individuals. At the end,
  however, we do get more generic, and it'll be difficult to create a
  concrete image.

- As you read each aspiration, try to form a sincere intention based
  on the wish. Be especially attentive to those you have difficulty
  wishing well.

- Make yourself comfortable, and follow the instructions. You may
  assume a traditional meditation position or simply sit on the sofa.
  You may find it helpful to close your eyes.

- In your mind, form an image of yourself, and wish for yourself the
  following: May I be well and happy. May I be well and happy. May
  I have no fears or sorrows. May I be healthy and free from illness.
  May I live calmly and peacefully.

- Now, imagine your parents, and make the following aspirations:
  May my parents be well and happy. May my parents be well and
  happy. May they have no fears or sorrows. May they be healthy and
  free from illness. May they live calmly and peacefully.

- If you have one, think of your spouse or life companion. May my
  spouse be well and happy. May my spouse be well and happy. May

he or she have no fears or sorrows. May he or she be healthy and free from illness. May my spouse live calmly and peacefully.

- If you have a child or children, hold their image before your mind. May my children be well and happy. May my children be well and happy. May they have no fears or sorrows. May they be healthy and free from illness. May my children live calmly and peacefully.

- Imagine one of your relatives, a brother or sister, aunt or uncle, or any family member to whom you're close. May my relatives be well and happy. May my relatives be well and happy. May they have no fears or sorrows. May they be healthy and free from illness. May my relatives live calmly and peacefully.

- Think of one of your older benefactors, a teacher or other elder. May my teachers and elders be well and happy. May my teachers and elders be well and happy. May they have no fears or sorrows. May they be healthy and free from illness. May my teachers and elders live calmly and peacefully.

- Consider a friend. This is a person for whom you feel great affection. May my friends be well and happy. May my friends be well and happy. May they have no fears or sorrows. May they be healthy and free from illness. May my friends live calmly and peacefully.

- Now, call before your mind a person for whom you have no strong feelings, a neutral person. Although you do not know this person well, you know that he or she shares a common bond in being human. May my acquaintance be well and happy. May my acquaintance be well and happy. May he or she have no fears or sorrows. May he or she be healthy and free from illness. May this person live calmly and peacefully.

- Imagine an enemy or person you strongly dislike. Although this person is an enemy, he or she is just like you—with pains and frustrations, desires and hopes. May my enemies be well and happy.

May my enemies be well and happy. May they have no fears or sorrows. May they be healthy and free from illness. May my enemies live calmly and peacefully.

- Consider all human beings. Dwell a moment on their pain and anguish. Suffering afflicts every one of us, and everyone wishes to be free of it. May all people be well and happy. May all people be well and happy. May they have no fears or sorrows. May they be healthy and free from illness. May all people live calmly and peacefully.

Corel Stock Photo Library.

Tenzin Gyatso, the 14th Dalai Lama, said: "If you want others to be happy, practice compassion. If you want to be happy, practice compassion."

- Now, think of all living beings, from the lowliest single-cell organisms to the highest forms of intelligence. Every one of them wants to live and be happy. May all living beings, everywhere and without exception, be well and happy. May all living beings, everywhere and without exception, be well and happy. May all living beings, everywhere and without exception, have no fears or sorrows. May all living beings, everywhere and without exception, be healthy and free from illness. May all living beings, everywhere and without exception, live calmly and peacefully.

Loving-Kindness Meditation

- Many people have a hard time believing that simply wishing can free others from fear, illness, and other forms of anguish. However, medical studies have been conducted that support the claim that prayer has a tangible, empirical effect on the health of those prayed for.

- Whether or not you believe in the effects of this practice, it is important to consider the fact that relieving a little of the hostility of just one person—yourself—will make that world a little better for everyone.

- Perhaps if your enemies were truly happy and free from suffering, then they wouldn't be your enemies. After all, what makes them such difficult people derives from their own struggle with dukkha— the very thing that makes you a difficult person for them. Plus, it's a little harder to get angry at someone for whom you've been wishing happiness.

- Loving-kindness meditation is a way to cultivate the mind and heart to produce wholesome actions. The practice doesn't, however, tell us in advance specific ways to act. Rather, the practice sensitizes us to the manifestations of suffering and prepares us to respond when the opportunity arises.

Important Term

metta meditation: An ancient practice that has long been the cornerstone for cultivating compassion in the Buddhist tradition. "Metta" is a Buddhist term that usually translates as "loving-kindness."

Questions to Consider

1. How is the well-being of others related to our personal happiness?

2. How is it possible to be compassionate toward another without feelings of affection?

3. Do you agree with the Buddha's contention that hostility cannot be ended with hostility?

Generosity—The Joy of Giving
Lecture 18

Many people that live in an affluent society own a lot of stuff—generic, inessential, space-consuming stuff. When you first acquired the material items you possess, they probably brought you a bit of pleasure—or maybe a lot of pleasure. Where is that pleasure now? Are you really happy with all that stuff? The Buddha said: "If you knew what I know about the power of generosity, you would not let a single meal go by without sharing it." Think of generosity as a way of exchanging your impermanent material goods for more lasting spiritual benefits.

Greed and Materialism

- Human beings seem to accumulate material items the way squirrels store up acorns for the winter. There was a time in our evolution as a species when collecting things conferred survival advantages: When resources were scarce, the more we had, the better we could protect ourselves against the onslaught of enemies, famine, or catastrophic weather.

- Eating copious quantities of food rich in sugar and fat served the same purpose; it helped us survive when we were uncertain when our next meal would be. In the midst of affluence, however, the evolutionary benefits we once gained from hoarding and the unrestricted consumption of sugar and fat seem now to have passed—but the old habits have not.

- Just as immoderately indulging our appetites for rich foods can be detrimental to our well-being, so too can be the acquisition of stuff. The mindfulness tradition regards our voracious appetite for wanting and accumulating inessential things to be a form of greed—one of the principal roots of dukkha.

- **Greed**, or self-centered desire for unnecessary things, is considered a defilement, a poison of the mind. It distorts our view of reality and leaves us unhappy. Whether or not we get what we want, selfish craving causes us to suffer.

- According to traditional Buddhist mythology, there is an entire realm of existence populated by beings that are consumed with greed. This is the realm of the hungry ghosts. The hungry ghosts are depicted as shadowy beings that are driven by their intense desire. They have enormous bellies but extremely narrow gullets and tiny mouths. No matter how much they try to eat, they can never consume enough to feel satisfied. When they drink, the liquid turns to fire, intensifying their thirst.

- The torture of the hungry ghosts derives not so much from the frustration of not getting what they want; they suffer because they cling to the things they mistakenly believe will bring them satisfaction and relief.

© Hemera/Thinkstock.

Many people that live in an affluent society own a lot of stuff that is inessential to their lives.

- The plight of the hungry ghosts closely parallels the lives of those of us who are overtaken by the defilement of greed. Like the hungry ghosts, the real problem of greedy people is our attachment to the idea that stuff will make us happy. The problem is not that there's something wrong with material things. Material things are fine and, to some extent, even necessary.

- The mindfulness tradition affirms the value of good food, adequate shelter, and a healthy body. The real issue we greedy people must face is the tremendous expectations we place on having stuff.

- Once we have provided for our basic needs, our craving continues unabated. Meeting our fundamental needs feels so good that we assume more of the same will make us feel even better.

- Despite that belief, the majority of us think that material acquisition is not really the avenue to happiness. Although many of us affirm this idea, we still surround ourselves with stuff and devote a vast quantity of our time and energy to the pursuit of things.

Beliefs versus Practices

- Although we claim to believe it, perhaps we haven't fully accepted the idea that the best things in life aren't material things. It sounds noble, and all the wisdom traditions tell us it's true, but it's very hard to embrace that claim wholeheartedly when the dominant message of our culture tells us just the opposite. It's extremely difficult to be out of step with the prevailing ethos of society.

- Perhaps we still harbor the idea that there really is something out there that will make us happy. It may be a secret belief that we hide even from our conscious awareness. Maybe we haven't truly grasped the fact that acquisition is unable to satisfy us. The roots of greed are very deep and require much effort to understand.

- Perhaps we continue with our greedy habits simply because we don't really know of any alternatives. Acquisition is so ingrained into us that we may feel bored without it.

- Whatever the reason, many of us often feel torn in opposite directions between our greedy behavior and our deeper aspirations—and we continue to suffer, partly from our selfish desires and partly from our guilt.

- The mindfulness approach to this problem follows the twofold path of seeking wisdom and practicing compassion. In the case of greed, seeking wisdom means deep insight into the transient and unsatisfying nature of the world and practicing compassion means cultivating generosity.

Mindfulness and Generosity

- The mindfulness tradition does not endorse a life of poverty and deprivation. It doesn't romanticize poverty, thinking that what the poor lack in material resources they make up in spiritual gains.

- Rather, the mindfulness tradition values simplicity. It recognizes that we must meet our basic material needs, but it also sees the danger of attachment to the world of things.

- The mindfulness tradition calmly and dispassionately recognizes that the ephemeral nature of our lives rules out any effort to find security or permanence in a world in constant change. It means we must stay on our guard to relax the tendency to latch onto things in the hope they will somehow satisfy our desires.

- As with other spiritual afflictions, the mindfulness tradition offers specific forms of practice to help neutralize the defilements of greed and attachment. The practice of generosity is the most potent antidote to greed. Generosity is fundamentally a state of mind that is manifested in particular acts of giving.

- On the simplest level, **generosity** is the willingness to give to others, but on a deeper level, generosity is the eagerness to relinquish anything that we feel is "ours." In this sense, generosity is a way to relax our tendency to become attached to things, including the principal cause of suffering: the illusion of the self.

- In the Buddhist world, generosity is one of the basic practices of the tradition. Long before Buddhists take up the disciplines of meditation, they are taught the value of *dana*, the word for generosity. As a formal practice in traditional Buddhist societies, *dana* takes the form of providing monks and nuns with food, clothing, and the basic necessities of life.

- Even beyond this, *dana* is understood as the custom of sharing with others. *Dana* practices in these cultures bring great joy to both the recipient and the giver. Families often spend days planning and preparing a single meal for the local monastics, and everyone works together to share the best of what they have with others.

- *Dana* practices are regarded as so joyful that just observing a generous act is believed to bring great happiness to the witness. In Buddhist mythology, the hungry ghosts are able to ease their torment not by eating, but by observing an act of generosity and experiencing the happiness it brings.

- By the same token, those of us who live like hungry ghosts can relieve the suffering of our incessant wanting by being generous and taking delight in the generosity of others.

- In the modern Western world, there are few opportunities for practicing *dana* in the traditional sense, but there are ample opportunities for observing it in other ways. The fundamental component in the practice of generosity is a reorientation of our thinking about wealth and giving.

- The mindfulness practice of generosity invites us to think about giving to another as a form of enrichment rather than as self-impoverishment. Consider generosity as the gift you not only give to others but to yourself as well. This is hard to do, of course, if you believe that the material world is more real or more important than the spiritual. Part of practicing generosity means relaxing that pervasive assumption.

- In addition, we don't need to attain a certain level of wealth to be generous. In fact, social research indicates that people toward the lower end of the economic scale tend to give away a greater proportion of what they have than those at the upper end.

Cultivating a Mind of Generosity

- Cultivating a mind of generosity—modest as it may seem—is a vital step in the direction of meeting the greater challenges of ensuring that the basic needs of everyone are met.

- These simple practices don't directly address the really grave issues of world hunger and the gross inequities between rich and poor, but they go a long way toward creating a mind sensitive to the needs of others and cautious about the seductions of greed.

- First, find one of your cherished possessions, and give it to someone who would appreciate it. Take time with this exercise; give it deep consideration. It doesn't have to be your most prized possession, but it should be an item you hold dear.

- Then, think about someone who would value having it. Perhaps you have a friend who has seen it and expressed appreciation for it. Then, on no particular occasion, give it to your friend. Be keenly attentive to the effects this action has on you, your friend, and your relationship.

- In addition, knowing what a sincere compliment does for us, we can imagine the goodwill it generates when we offer praise to another. Giving compliments is such an easy thing to do—if we can only remember to do it and do it with a sincere heart. Trying to make it a habit helps, but complimenting out of habit has potential pitfalls.

- Simply praising someone out of custom is disingenuous and reinforces an unwholesome state of mind, but one can help shape a mind of generosity by sincerely seeking to discover the good qualities in someone else and reflecting them back to the individual as a gift.

- It's essential, of course, that the gift of a compliment is offered with sincerity and without expectation of anything in return. A truly generous spirit gives freely—without strings attached.

- As the practice of complimenting illustrates, simply giving to others is not sufficient for cultivating true generosity. As with other forms of compassion, generosity must be exercised with wisdom. We have to maintain mindful vigilance about our motivations and practice responsible stewardship over our resources.

Important Terms

dana: The Buddhist word for generosity.

generosity: The willingness to give to others; on a deeper level, it is the eagerness to relinquish anything that one might feel is a possession.

greed: The self-centered desire for unnecessary things; it is considered to be a poison of the mind because it distorts one's view of reality and leaves one unhappy.

Questions to Consider

1. What drives the Western world's obsession with acquiring and having material objects?

2. How does practicing mindfulness help to foster a spirit of generosity?

3. Consider the material object that would be most difficult for you to part with. Why would it be hard to let it go?

Speech—Training the Tongue
Lecture 19

The link between the quality of language and the caliber of behavior is widely recognized; our words have an undeniable effect on the way we think and act. The skillful use of language involves not simply refraining from using false speech but also giving mindful attention to what we say and how we say it. Thoughtful, wholesome language can be the bearer of our compassion. The book of Proverbs reminds us: "Thoughtless words cut like a sword. But the tongue of the wise brings healing."

Wholesome Speech and Skillful Communication

- The Buddha devoted much of his teaching to the practice of skillful communication and offered very cogent ideas to guide our efforts to use language in the most beneficial ways possible.

- The Buddha taught that skillful speech should be truthful, compassionate, gentle, and edifying. When our words have all these qualities, we can know that our use of language is wholesome and conducive to the end of suffering. However, attaining these qualities is no mean feat.

- Speaking the truth is the basic condition for skillful speech, yet it is a fundamental qualification that many of us find difficult to observe. Most of us are quite capable of telling flat-out falsehoods if we think we can benefit by them, and some of us would tell them frequently if we thought we wouldn't be caught.

- Even when we don't go so far as to tell bald-faced lies, we often embellish and stretch the truth to suit our own desires. These forms of false speech can become so habitual that we even fail to recognize when they leave our lips.

The Buddha's Criteria for Wholesome Speech

- Because we're often mindless about the truthfulness of our utterances, it behooves us to pay careful attention to the content of what we say. The Buddha prescribed a simple procedure for ensuring we're speaking the truth.

Truthful Speech

- As a matter of practice, we can carefully monitor our words with mindfulness by paying attention to make sure our words comport with what we know to be true and by refraining from pretending we know when in fact we don't. We can use that same practice to help us better understand our propensity to speak falsely.

- After you observe yourself deviating from or exaggerating the truth, use your sitting practice to examine the antecedent causes underlying what you've said. If we look diligently, we'll usually find the illusion of the self lurking in there somewhere.

- The fear that often motivates a falsehood can arise from the belief that we need to appear a certain way, which is, of course, a basic expression of the ego. Likewise, embellishing the truth can serve to make ourselves seem more interesting and perhaps more important than we really are.

- As you're investigating the causes for any instances of false speech, reflect as well on the consequences. Study the effects of failing to be truthful. Take special note of the ways that dishonesty causes you to suffer.

- Whereas truthfulness is a necessary condition for skillful speech, it is not by any means the sole criterion. Just because something is truthful does not mean we should say it. Truth must be spoken compassionately. The manner in which truth is communicated is of great importance in the practice of skillful speech.

- To the provision of truthfulness, the Buddha added that wholesome speech should be delivered in a timely manner in a way that benefits the listener. For instance, we sometimes find ourselves in conversations when we have a piece of truthful information to offer, but we recognize that this particular occasion is not the best time or place to share it.

- It might be something that is better imparted privately with the person it concerns or perhaps it's a point that needs to be said when the

The effort to make hurtful assertions under the veil of truth still has the objective to harm.

individual it concerns is in the proper frame of mind to receive it. In any event, it's best to maintain silence until conditions are better suited for compassionate communication.

- The Buddha made a point of saying, however, that compassionate communication does not depend on whether or not one's words would be welcomed by the hearer. If what one had to say were true, beneficial, and timely, the Buddha recommended that one speak— whether or not others would find those words agreeable.

- In short, being compassionate does not mean saying what others want to hear. It means speaking the truth in a kind of way that can help bring relief from suffering. Sometimes, the recipient may find even a compassionately delivered truth unwelcome, yet for the sake of being compassionate, one must find a way to say it.

- When hard, truthful messages have to be given, it's crucial to be clear about intent. Always ask yourself: Why am I saying this? What am I really trying to accomplish with these words? It's easy for us to fool ourselves when it comes to conversing with others—just as it's easy to fool ourselves in our internal dialogue.

- There are those who believe that the truth must be spoken regardless of consequences. These are those who think of themselves as brutally honest, and they consider their candor a noble quality. Often, however, those who pride themselves on their brutal honesty seem to get more pleasure from being brutal than from being honest.

Compassionate Speech

- Efforts to make hurtful assertions under the veil of truth are nothing more than what the Buddha called **malicious speech**. A malicious statement may be either true or false, but its objective is to harm.

- Malicious speech has been around since shortly after the first human being uttered the first word. Lately, however, it seems to have gained a new dimension with the explosion of electronic media, which has created a distance between writers and the effects of their words.

- The personal distance, the opportunity for immediate response, and the frequent anonymity afforded by the Internet is a virtual invitation for many of us to disregard the principles of propriety and vent our spleens shamelessly.

Gentle Speech

- The Buddha's third criterion for wholesome speech is gentleness. Our words should be truthful, beneficial, and timely, and they should be spoken in a mild manner. This characterization thus excludes malicious speech and what the Buddha called harsh speech.

- Malicious speech has the clear intent of hurting others, but **harsh speech** may be hurtful without any real intent to be so. Harsh speech is usually thoughtless, although it can also be malicious at times.

- Harsh speech includes profanity, sarcasm, and shouting. Essentially, harsh speech is the use of language that shows little or no regard for the feelings of others.

- Avoiding harsh speech is the negative aspect of speaking gently. The positive side involves choosing kind words and speaking them clearly and soothingly. Gentle speech means offering sincere compliments to others, helping to facilitate constructive discussion, and listening mindfully to what others have to say.

- Gentleness of speech can also mean keeping silent so that others may be heard or simply to allow high emotions to settle. The equanimity that we cultivate as we continue mindfulness practice helps us speak our words with mildness.

Edifying Speech

- Finally, the Buddha urges that our speech serve a constructive purpose. This is what is meant when we say that our words should edify. Unless our words work to provide us some real benefit, it's best to keep quiet. When a wise word can help, though—when it can ease suffering or open us to new insight—speaking is a blessing.

- Like gentleness, edifying speech has both a negative and a positive aspect. The negative side is those expressions of language that are best to avoid. The Buddha called these forms of speech **idle chatter**—the verbal equivalent of stuff, or unnecessary material possessions. It's generic, inessential language whose basic purpose is to fill airspace.

- Idle chatter often arises because silence seems so threatening. It's interesting that the English language has a great many words to describe idle chatter. They include: babble, blab, drivel, gab, jabber, jive, prattle, yakking, twaddle, and running off at the mouth.

- The most invidious form of idle chatter goes by the name of gossip, which is so pervasive that it's hard to imagine life without it. It seems almost natural to want to know about the intimate details of the lives of others.

- The phenomenon of gossip is complex, serving many functions and deriving from many causes. Certainly, part of the reason gossip is so appealing is that it lets individuals monitor social situations so they can relate to others accordingly. Sharing gossip with friends may even be a form of bonding. At least in a few ways, then, gossip may serve some important purposes.

- The perilous aspect of gossip, however, is the way it easily becomes vicious. Even when information is true, gossip has a way of shaping the truth in a negative fashion.

- Deep within most of us is the hidden—and sometimes not so hidden—capacity to enjoy hearing about the misfortunes of others, even those to whom we're close.

- What's really sad, of course, is the way that malicious gossip can cause suffering. There is now growing evidence to indicate that many teen suicides in this country have been prompted, at least in part, by vicious rumors spread by word of mouth and especially through social networks on the Internet. Perhaps less apparent is the effect of gossiping on those who perpetuate it.

- While it may be true that gossip serves some useful social functions, we ought to give thought to whether or not those functions might be better served by other, more benign means. Even when it is not malicious, idle chatter in its various forms can be a colossal waste of precious time.

Meditation and Wholesome Speech

- Wholesome speech, as taught in the Buddhist mindfulness tradition, is truthful, compassionate, gentle, and edifying. We can remember these qualities if we think of them as simple questions to ask ourselves before we speak: Why do I want to say this? Is what I want to say completely true? Will what I say result in benefit or harm? Is now the right time to say it? How may I say it to be most beneficial and effective?

- Practicing loving-kindness meditation predisposes us to being more compassionate, cultivating a frame of mind in which matters such as the effect of our words are already a prime concern. Long before we engage in conversation, our hearts are attuned to speaking compassionately.

- Sitting and walking meditation also play important roles in shaping skillful speech. These practices, of course, sharpen our skills of observation and moment-to-moment awareness. Using these techniques allows us give close attention not only to what is said but also to how we respond emotionally, mentally, and physically.

- A refined ability to monitor our own internal states makes it possible for us to avoid knee-jerk reactions and provides us with enough mental space to be more deliberate about how we respond.

- Getting to this level of self-awareness and discipline, of course, requires a great deal of practice, but learning to create a spacious mind is a powerful ally in learning to use speech skillfully. It is also an especially valuable technique in working with anger.

Important Terms

harsh speech: Speech that may be hurtful without any real intent to be so; the use of language that shows little or no regard for the feelings of others. It is usually thoughtless and includes profanity, sarcasm, and shouting.

idle chatter: Generic, inessential language whose basic purpose is to fill airspace; it is the verbal equivalent of unnecessary material possessions.

malicious speech: The Buddhist term for the practice of making hurtful assertions under the veil of truth. A malicious statement may be either true or false, but its objective is to harm.

1. What are your usual first reactions to an abusive comment? Anger, fear, or shock? What do you usually do, say, and think? Are your responses as skillful as you would like? If not, how can more skillful means be cultivated?

2. What qualities of wholesome speech—truthful, compassionate, gentle, and edifying—are most difficult for you to observe and why?

Anger—Cooling the Fires of Irritation
Lecture 20

Anger is a complex human experience involving every feature of our being: our bodies, our minds, and our emotions. The mindfulness tradition regards anger as an unwholesome state of being that is both a cause and a manifestation of dukkha. Despite its negative quality, however, the tradition also sees anger as a potential ally in the realization of freedom from suffering. If we know how to handle it skillfully, anger has much to teach us and can point the way to new insights and more wholesome ways of living.

Anger and Suffering

- **Anger** can be defined as the feeling of displeasure, usually accompanied by antagonism. It encompasses a wide range of experiences from simple irritation and annoyance to rage and fury.

- Most of the time, we experience anger as unpleasant. Our heart rate and blood pressure can increase dramatically, and our muscles can become tense and spasmodic. Our emotions become raw, and our facial expression may contort. We are unable to think clearly.

- Anger can also be dangerous. Because it clouds our thoughts, it can incite us to act in ways we later regret. In a state of anger, we can easily say and do hurtful things and even take the life of another.

- Anger is a cause of much of the world's suffering. The mindfulness tradition reminds us, furthermore, that anger itself is a form of suffering. Those who inflict pain out of anger are also the sufferers of its torment.

- Like other forms of suffering, anger is closely connected to **attachment**, the way we cling to the various items of our experience as if we can't live without them. Anger often arises when something to which we're attached is threatened or is taken away from us.

- Although anger is considered an unwholesome state because it causes and manifests suffering, the experience of anger itself is not really a problem—or, perhaps, it doesn't have to be a problem.

- Anger is nothing more than an unpleasant feeling coupled with negative thoughts and certain bodily responses. The real problem with anger is how we react to those unpleasant feelings, thoughts, and sensations.

Anger and Mindlessness

- In mindlessness, we're liable to react to anger one of two basic ways. The first is to suppress the anger—to deny it and pretend it's not there. We can get so good at this technique that it becomes automatic, and we're not even aware of it.

- The other basic reaction is to express anger immediately. Like the subjective experience of anger, the expression of anger can take a wide range of forms. The reflexive expression of anger can also become habitual.

- Both ways of reacting to anger are usually conditioned by our upbringing and other circumstances, and both have potentially hazardous consequences. The suppression of anger may allow to us to feel composed and to avoid conflict—for a while, but this strategy doesn't work for long.

- Anger that is not given attention does not go away. Eventually, unacknowledged anger may turn to rage or cynicism, erupt in violent acts, or cast us into a pit of depression and despair.

- The reflexive expression of anger tends to be a more acceptable reaction in our culture, especially for men, and it's even endorsed by some schools of psychotherapy.

Anger and Mindfulness

- From the mindfulness point-of-view, the expression of anger—whether by word or deed—often ends up reinforcing negative states of mind, and it fails to address anger's deeper causes. Just as suppressing anger may afford a temporary respite from its unpleasantness, so too may expressing it.

- Neither suppression nor expression is genuinely effective at removing the potential perils of anger or its root causes. Hostility begets more hostility.

- With practice, it's possible to find a way beyond automatically suppressing anger or reflexively expressing it. The techniques for dealing with anger more appropriately are founded directly on the basic methods of meditation.

Responding to Anger Skillfully

- The first step in the process of responding skillfully to anger when it arises is being able to know when you're angry. Many of us simply cannot identify anger as it occurs.

- Meditation is an important instrument in learning to identify anger. Of key significance is the skill of nonjudgmental observation, the basic technique of watching what happens as it happens.

- In identifying anger, the skills we gain in the body scan meditation can help us monitor how our physical natures are responding in a difficult situation. Try to note the patterns of your physical responses that coordinate with the feelings of displeasure that suggest anger.

- Identifying anger is the first step. The second is accepting it. Because it can be such an unpleasant state, we often treat anger as we do other unwanted experiences: We try to distance ourselves from it as rapidly as possible.

- At this stage of aversion, our conditioned reflexes usually come into play. We immediately suppress or express our feelings as a way to get rid of them. Both reactions intend to accomplish the same thing: to bring relief to the unwelcome experience of displeasure.

- Mindfulness practice encourages us to approach all our experiences—wanted and unwanted—with equanimity. We try neither to cling to nor run away from our experiences, regardless of their quality.

- The aversion that results in the reflexive suppression or expression of anger, however, disturbs that equanimity. Rather than seeking to eliminate the unpleasantness of anger, the equanimous approach is to allow and accept it. We might even say we should welcome it.

- However, we must also be careful here. Acceptance doesn't mean that we necessarily want anger; that could be a form of desire that is just as dangerous as aversion. Anger can still be an unwanted experience—even when you accept it.

- Acceptance is simply the willingness to be attentive to our anger to see what it wants. Just observe and treat it compassionately. This allows you to experience anger as fully as possibly. The more completely you can feel anger, the less you will fear it. When we become familiar with anger, we're less apt to try to eliminate it when it arises.

- It is crucial to realize, however, that feeling anger is not the same as acting on it. Recognizing this distinction creates the mental spaciousness that allows us to be more conscious about how we choose to respond.

- In the mindless state, we react to anger reflexively, without conscious choice, but mindfulness allows us to make a deliberate decision about the course of action we should take in the face of anger.

- As we noted when discussing skillful speech, just because our anger may urge us to respond to an insult with another insult does not mean we have to do it. We're not obliged to follow this impulsive prompting.

- Instead, we can allow angry thoughts and sensations to arise and fall away, giving us the time to consider a more appropriate response. We may need to take time away from the heat of the moment to reflect on a wise response.

- It may be that after fully experiencing your anger and assessing your options, you choose to speak sharply. You might even return insult for insult. The difference is that you have made a choice and have not reacted by impulse.

- When you create space for reflection, you will be far less likely to act in a hostile way. Over time, the insights you gain through meditation and compassion exercises will reveal that antagonistic responses are never the most suitable ones.

© Digital Vision/Thinkstock.

- In rare instances, we might decide that the appropriate response to anger is to cause bodily harm to another person. What can make such a response appropriate is when it does not arise from self-centered desires and is not carried out with hostility.

Anger and Meditation

- Meditation not only helps us deal with our anger as it arises; it can also help us

If you have difficulty knowing if you're angry, giving attention to your body is a good place to start.

cultivate a mind that is slow to anger, thus preparing us for anger before it arises.

- After practicing meditation for a significant period of time, you may begin to discover that you're less prone to getting angry, even though you've made no particular efforts to manage your anger. This occurs because our state of mind is an essential factor in determining whether or not we become angry.

- A properly cared for mind is less apt to respond to certain situations with anger—or, if it does, the degree of anger can be greatly lessened. Caring for the mind means giving it moment-to-moment attention, making an effort to keep thoughts wholesome, creating a mind of non-attachment, practicing moral integrity, and keeping the body as healthy as possible.

- Thus, one of the best ways for dealing with anger is to prevent it from arising in the first place by cultivating a mental field where it is difficult for the seeds of anger to germinate.

Studying Individual Patterns of Anger

- The process of caring for the mind is greatly enhanced by studying individual patterns of anger. Different things make different people angry.

- As you practice sitting meditation, you can study your anger experience. Make note of the things that contribute to your anger. Think about not only the things that make you mad but also the less obvious conditioning factors that might contribute to the provocation of anger.

- Anger has a lot to tell us about ourselves. Try to look beneath the anger and see what's there; it's often some kind of fear. Like pain, anger is a signal that something is wrong and needs to change.

- If we know how to experience it skillfully, anger can help us to make wholesome changes in ourselves and the society in which we live. The key is to not allow anger to develop into hostility or hatred; when that happens, anger becomes dangerous.

Working with Deep-Seated Anger

- Although we usually try to distance ourselves from anger as quickly as possible, sometimes we may find ourselves holding onto it. We can be averse to anger, but we can also get attached to it.

- Attachments to anger often manifest as grudges that we can carry for a long, long time. Life hurts us all, but some of us choose to dwell on those hurts and periodically renew their pain. As the Buddha recognized, nursing a grudge only serves to injure the one who bears it.

- The mindfulness approach to these old, festering forms of anger is forgiveness. Think of forgiveness as a form of relinquishment. To relinquish, in this sense, is to release whatever power anger holds over us.

- Forgiveness, in this sense, is rarely easy or quick. Because of its difficulty, forgiveness has to be practiced; it's less an act than a way of living. True forgiveness often comes only at the end of an inner struggle, and sometimes, it's a long one. Be wary of forgiving too quickly.

- We forgive others not so much to make them feel better, although it might. Rather, we forgive to be free—to liberate ourselves from the destructive power of anger and hatred. Holding a grudge rarely causes harm to the object of our anger, but it causes us a great deal.

- As the thoughts and feelings of anger arise, we observe them, acknowledge them, and allow them to pass away. We practice loving-kindness meditation, exercise empathy, and recognize the futility of seeking revenge. We also remember our own propensity to make mistakes. We repeat these techniques until our anger has been freed and we have been freed from its bondage.

anger: The feeling of displeasure, usually accompanied by antagonism; it encompasses a wide range of experiences from simple irritation and annoyance to rage and fury.

attachment: The way in which people cling to the various items of their experiences as if they can't live without them.

1. What patterns do you discern in your experiences of anger? What sorts of things evoke your anger? Do your reactions to anger follow specifiable habits? What do these patterns suggest about your beliefs about yourself?

2. In what ways does mindfulness offer more wholesome ways to respond to anger?

Pain—Embracing Physical Discomfort
Lecture 21

Pain, like everything else, is transient. The two guided meditations that we'll experience in this lecture are designed to give you an experiential acquaintance with the basic techniques for working with pain mindfully. These exercises will help you release your anger toward pain and accept your situation in moments of pain. As a result of these practices, you might be less inclined to feel pity for yourself by thinking your situation of pain is unfair. Throughout the world, at every moment of every hour, millions of people endure great pain. Pain is a fact of life.

Responding to Pain

- To be embodied means to be vulnerable to pain. Because of our physical nature, we are susceptible to viruses and bacteria, head-on collisions, slipping on icy sidewalks, random violence, heart attacks, beestings, and tsunamis.

- Even if by some miracle we escape the pain associated with disease and injury, we must still face the pain of getting old and watching our body wear out. Pain is a fact of life.

- Our typical response to pain is aversion. We simply don't want it, and we seek to avoid painful experiences as much as possible. As we've noted, however, aversion is an unwise strategy for living.

- Because pain is a fact of life, feverishly trying to separate ourselves from it is tantamount to separating ourselves from life itself. Instead, it is important to accept pain and other unwanted experiences as part of the greater affirmation of living life to its fullest extent.

- Mindfulness practice is a way to teach ourselves how to accept life as it is—in both its sweetness and its dreadfulness. Because pain is an immense, and often terrifying, component of life's dreadfulness, learning to respond to it in a wholesome way is an essential part of fully embracing life.

Pain versus Suffering

- Central to the mindfulness approach to pain is grasping the distinction between pain and suffering. In this tradition, pain is understood to be a name we give to a range of unpleasant sensations because what constitutes pain is highly subjective.

- Pain is usually an indication that some facet of our being requires attention. In those cases, of course, we should seek out any medical intervention that may reduce or eliminate the sensations of pain and address its root causes.

- In principle, the mindfulness tradition has no reluctance about using medication or other medical procedures to diminish pain, but it does urge us to use wisdom when doing so.

- Sometimes medication used to diminish pain can be addictive or can hinder us from seeking out the deeper causes of our distress. Sometimes medication and intervention is simply ineffective. In these cases, coping with pain by mindfulness is helpful.

- Mindfulness is perhaps an even greater ally in dealing with suffering. Suffering in this context occurs when the mind responds negatively to the sensations it identifies as pain. It's not always easy to distinguish pain from suffering.

- This distinction is important because the mindfulness tradition considers pain to be inevitable—an inescapable part of life as we know it. Suffering, on the other hand, is regarded as optional.

- In the case of pain, what generates suffering is resistance, which means wanting this moment to be other than it actually is. Resisting pain can take many forms, including responding with fear and panic, with anger, and with hatred—all of which are types of aversion.

- The more we resist the pain that is undeniably present, the greater our suffering—and the greater our suffering, the more likely we are to act in unskillful ways.

- The key to diminishing the suffering that we usually connect to physical pain is acceptance. Acceptance means confronting unwanted pain without fear or hatred. In the following guided exercises, we'll begin to work with our pain by learning to accept it for what it is, to greet it with compassion, and inquire about what it may have to teach us.

Preparing for Guided Meditations

- The following guided meditations offer instructions on ways to work with pain. Feel free to participate whether or not you are currently experiencing pain. It's beneficial to learn to work with milder forms of physical distress before trying to apply mindfulness techniques to pain's stronger manifestations.

- Before you begin these exercises, remember that it's important to let go of any attachments you may have to attaining specific results with these exercises—especially because pain is a complex phenomenon, and our responses to it are deeply conditioned.

- Accordingly, we shouldn't expect significant changes initially. The results of these exercises may become apparent only after a significant period of practice.

- Furthermore, meditating on pain may never remove the unpleasant sensations you must live with. That is simply an unrealistic hope. However, scientific studies do support the view that diligent mindfulness practice can significantly ameliorate the suffering associated with pain.

Pain and Awareness

- In the same way as you would prepare for sitting practice or a body scan, choose whichever posture you find most comfortable and most conducive to alertness. As always, make sure your environment is quiet and free from distractions.

- This first exercise is designed simply to direct your attention to the pain and allow you to feel the sensation as much as possible. Rather than trying to take our mind off the pain, in this meditation, we'll be bringing our awareness right into the painful sensation and staying with it.

- First, make sure your body is in its proper position. Make yourself as comfortable as possible, but stay alert. You may keep your eyes open or closed, as you prefer.

- Begin by taking several deep breaths, and gently bring your awareness to the sensation of breathing. With each inhale and each exhale, allow your body to settle into a deeper state of relaxation. As your body becomes more at ease, your attention becomes more focused on this present moment.

- Now, allow your attention to range throughout your body and let it alight on that part that seems most in distress at this moment. It may be an area of mild discomfort or a part that seems to be in a fair amount of pain. Once you've made your selection, stay with that area for the remainder of the exercise.

- Let your awareness approach the area slowly and cautiously. You may be a bit apprehensive about focusing your attention on this location. Sometimes we're afraid to look at painful places too closely for fear that we might be overwhelmed by unpleasant sensations or by frightening thoughts about what might be causing the pain. If you detect this sort of resistance, softly note it to yourself, let it go, and proceed.

- Your purpose is simply to observe. You're making no judgments about the pain. You have no intention to change it in any way. You neither want it to leave nor to stay. You merely want the pain to be what it is and to give it the attention it deserves.

- Let your attention come as close to the pain as possible. If your resistance to getting close becomes too great, you can always escort your awareness back to the breath and try later. When you're ready, give the painful area your full awareness and observe it with kindhearted curiosity. Silently note your observations.

- Try to define the region that feels painful. Try to gain a sense of the contours of the painful area. Observe how deeply the pain goes into your body. Imagine a three-dimensional model of your pain.

- Then, consider how you might describe the quality of your pain. Pain is experienced in a wide range of ways, and its descriptive vocabulary is immense. Choose the words that make the most sense to you. It may be, however, simply indescribable.

- Now, examine the dynamics of the pain. Most of the time, pain is changing, although it's not always easy to detect this change. Consider if the pain is fluctuating in its intensity.

- For the next few moments, simply keep your awareness on the painful area, and remain keenly observant of the sensations you feel. This time, avoid labeling the sensations and simply feel them.

© iStockphoto/Thinkstock.

The key to diminishing the suffering that we usually connect to physical pain is acceptance.

- Now, try to become aware of your awareness of the pain. That may sound a little paradoxical, but it can be done. Simply watch yourself as you're observing your painful sensations. As you do so, see if your awareness is in pain.

- If you can become an observer of your own awareness, you may discover a place where there is no pain. Dwelling in this awareness may help mitigate the painful sensations in your body.

- You're no longer a person in pain but someone observing a person in pain. Being in this observing space may allow you to see that your pain is not you, and you are not your pain. Staying in this particular place of awareness is not easy, and it takes practice to do so—just as it takes practice to remain focused on the breath.

- Now, let's return to the breath and draw this exercise to a close. Let your attention come back to your breathing for a few moments.

- Reflect on your experience with the practice we've just completed. Did you notice any initial resistance to turning your attention to the painful area in your body? If so, what thoughts or emotions lay underneath that resistance? If you were able to give your pain a fuller attention, how did you mind respond?

Pain and Thinking

- In this second exercise, we'll incorporate more of the thinking process into the practice. It's not necessary to perform this exercise immediately after the one we've just completed; you can spend more time working with the first exercise before trying this one.

- First, take your position in the posture of your choice. Begin as you always do by relaxing your body and focusing on your inhalations and exhalations. Direct your attention to your breath, and stay attentive to what is occurring moment by moment.

- Now, permit your awareness to range over your entire body, and let it come to rest at the place of greatest discomfort. Be attentive to this location and observe the character of the sensations there as you did before.

- After you've had a chance to be aware of these sensations, turn your attention to your thoughts. Has the attention you've given this area of your body generated any mental commentary? If so, notice the character of those thoughts.

- As you become aware of these thoughts, try to relinquish them. See if you can distinguish the sensations from your thoughts about the sensations. Try to anchor your awareness in the bodily sensations alone. If a thought arises, simply observe and let it fall away.

- After some practice, see if remaining focused on the sensations and dropping thoughts alleviates the discomfort.

- Now, let's return to the breath and draw this exercise to a close. Let your attention come back to your breathing for a few moments.

- The intention of the exercise we've just concluded was to investigate the role of thinking in the experience of pain. Essentially, we wanted to see if our conditioned thought patterns worsened the unpleasant sensations we call pain.

- Next time, try to minimize any negative commentary to see if that helps. Imagine experiencing the sensation without labeling it as pain. How do you think that would change your experience?

Questions to Consider

1. Examine your history with pain. What attitudes toward pain have you developed? What habits have you created for coping with it?

2. In your experience, which strategy do you find more helpful: giving full attention to the manifestation of pain or trying to divert attention away from it?

Grief—Learning to Accept Loss
Lecture 22

Mindfully working with grief essentially means removing any obstacles that might impede the natural course of grieving. In other words, grief is an invitation to welcome our experience with equanimity—without fear or aversion. It is to be open to whatever grief brings to us and to allow ourselves to experience that fully. Grief is not always predictable, and it doesn't follow a set timetable or path. It has to be allowed to happen on its own, taking its own good time.

Grief and Loss

- **Grieving** is the process of coming to terms with loss in our lives. Almost from the very moment we're born, we have to deal with loss. Newborns come into the world having lost the warmth and comfort of their mothers' wombs, and from that instant onward, life can seem like a string of losses.

- Some losses, of course, are greater than others. Losing a loved one to death is more significant and more distressing for most people than losing a mere material object, but the loss of anything can cause suffering and can require the process of grieving to help us adjust.

- Take a moment to reflect on the losses in your own life. Almost certainly, you've lost someone close to you to death—a parent or grandparent, a spouse, a friend, or a relative.

- We endure loss through means other than death, of course. We can lose our jobs and our life savings. We can see cherished possessions stolen or accidentally broken. Our friends may leave because of a quarrel, or we may leave them when we move away to embark on a new career.

- In the American courtship system, one can undergo a series of romantic breakups before finding a spouse. Even after marriage, one faces a 50% chance of divorce. As we age, we may begin to recognize that the youthful dreams we had long held are unlikely to materialize.

- These losses can cause us to suffer greatly, but for the significant losses in our lives, we need to grieve, and mindfulness practice can help facilitate our grief skillfully.

- Grief is a natural healing process that has several identifiable dimensions. Often, these aspects of the process are referred to as stages, a notion that suggests that grief follows a predictable, linear course as we come to terms with our loss.

- The typology of grief proposed by Elisabeth Kübler-Ross notes that grief sequentially progresses through the stages of denial, anger, bargaining, depression, and acceptance. While grief certainly can include these phases and experiences, it may be misleading, and potentially harmful, to suggest that grief is predictable or follows a specific timetable.

Practice breathing meditation in a graveyard. Notice and appreciate the way the idea of death affects you.

- Each person grieves in different ways. There may be times when grief includes anger and sadness and other experiences, but the experiences may not come in a predictable sequence, and there may be no sharp divisions between these stages.

- The mindfulness approach to grief is not to usher us through various stages so that we might hasten onward to the final goal of acceptance. Rather, mindfulness practice can be used to ensure that we accept and fully experience whatever the process of grief brings us.

- Mindfulness assists the grieving process by helping us acknowledge and accept the universality and inevitability of loss. Having to give up what we have is unavoidable. Throughout our lives, things are taken away from us—sometimes with our consent and sometimes without.

- Resisting necessary losses, of course, can cause us to suffer. The mindfulness insight into the impermanence of all reality helps ease our resistance to living in a world where ultimately everything we hold dear will have to be relinquished.

Easing the Suffering of Grief

- Being aware of the universality and inevitability of loss—and realizing your solidarity with everyone else—implies that we are all well advised to begin to prepare for grief now. Why wait?

- Throughout our lives, almost on a daily basis, we are given ample opportunities to practice mindfully coping with loss. These occasions are chances to remind ourselves of the nature of impermanence and of the potential hazards of becoming attached to transient things.

- Remembering the transience of all life helps us to avoid developing unhealthy attachments that can cause us to suffer, but how does mindfulness help us cope with the loss of those things to which we have already become attached?

- Quite simply, it's no different from the way we handle any other unwanted experience we might have, including anger and pain. It involves acknowledging, accepting, and letting go.

- Mindfulness is of greatest benefit in the grieving process in keeping us focused in the present moment, the place we can fully feel the pain of loss. Loss of something important in our lives almost inevitably provokes us to worry about how to fill that void and to face the future. These are absolutely legitimate concerns, and they must be faced.

- Inordinate attention to apprehensions about the future, however, can also hinder the process of grieving, which requires momentarily setting aside these anxieties and being completely aware of our experience in the present.

- During the period of grief, mindfulness meditation can provide a deliberate opportunity for attending to the present. As we discovered in our conversations about anger and pain, fully experiencing what we find in each moment is the precondition for thinking and acting wisely.

- Practicing deliberate acts of self-compassion is also essential to grieving. Being self-compassionate during these periods not only means relaxing our usual tendencies toward self-judgment and criticism, but it also means being open to the expressions of compassion from others.

The Beloved Teacup

Even Zen masters have to be reminded of our attachment to objects and how to cope with loss.

In a Zen monastery several centuries ago, a young monk accidently broke his master's favorite antique teacup while cleaning. When he heard his master approach, he quickly gathered the pieces and put them behind his back. Then, he cleverly asked the master, "Sir, why must people die?" The master answered, "It's natural. Everything has a finite lifespan, and everything must die." Then, the novice produced the broken teacup and told his master, "It was time for your cup to die."

- Bearing in mind one's solidarity with others in grief is one way to ease our suffering; another is to bear in mind the serendipitous nature of life.

- **Serendipity** is the word for the phenomenon of discovering pleasant things not sought for. Part of the surprising and unpredictable quality of existence is the way that, sometimes, things can turn out better than we imagined or hoped.

- Because our foresight is so greatly limited, we're well advised not to rush to judgments about the events that happen to us. Remembering that we really do not know what the future holds for us, except the certainty of death, can often ease the anxieties we have about the future. We fear the worst, but often what turns out is for the best.

Dealing with Staggering Losses

- What do we do with losses that seem staggering, altogether outside the realm of normal human experience? There are times when people lose almost everything. One only has to think of earthquakes, tsunamis, hurricanes, genocides, and terrorist events—disasters whose horrors are difficult to comprehend and to integrate into our ordinary experience of life.

- Perhaps you may be able to understand such staggering events by appealing to the providence of a God or to the belief in rebirth or reincarnation—in which cases such massive suffering can somehow be redeemed and ameliorated.

- If you are hesitant to make such metaphysical claims, it makes it more difficult to put such losses in a comprehensive framework. Sometimes it seems that the only thing these disasters are good for is giving the survivors some perspective—which is of course no consolation to the victims—and perhaps the motivation to be more compassionate.

- These are times when ritual may come to our aid. Whatever our faith or culture, joining with others to share our grief—moving through the familiar elements of a ceremony and sharing words that have been spoken by others in our situation for generations—can help us keep in mind that this is part of our human lot and always has been.

- Here's where your own suffering can be of use to you: Many people find it's not until they have had to cope with setbacks of their own that they are truly able to have compassion for others.

- For as long as we're met with nothing but success—warm friendships, loving family, rewarding job—we're likely to think that all good things have come to us because we deserve them.

- Only when we experience some losses ourselves do we realize we had less control over events than we had believed. It's humbling and disillusioning, in the best sense of the word; it helps us rid ourselves of whatever illusions of permanence and control we may have been holding.

- Many mindfulness practitioners eventually come to see such losses as supports for meditation. It may be going too far to say these problems are actually welcomed, but once you have begun to use the tools of mindfulness in your daily life, it's almost certainly true that you will at least see your problems as opportunities for gaining a more intimate knowledge of the way your mind works.

- If you practice developing skillful means with life's everyday challenges, you'll be able to react more skillfully when the greater losses come to you, as they inevitably will. You'll understand that you're not being singled out for suffering—you're just having a life.

Important Terms

grieving: The process of coming to terms with loss in life.

serendipity: The word for the phenomenon of discovering pleasant things not sought for. Part of the surprising and unpredictable quality of existence is the way that, sometimes, things can turn out better than imagined.

Questions to Consider

1. Reflect on your experiences with grief. Did they follow a particular, specifiable pattern? What losses have caused you the greatest grief? Are there losses you still grieve?

2. Throughout the day, notice the times you experience loss—no matter how small. It may be staining your favorite shirt, losing the perfect parking spot, or being outbid on eBay. Notice your reactions to these losses. Use these experiences to deepen your practice with grief and your acceptance of impermanence.

Finitude—Living in the Face of Death
Lecture 23

There is great value in fully confronting our fear of death and contemplating it deliberately as a way to free ourselves from its bonds and to live our lives with greater appreciation for every moment we have. It is difficult to face our deaths—to imagine our lives ending—but it is precisely because of its impermanence that we value life so dearly. If we are able to live the present moment completely, accepting that all things are impermanent, we can have fulfillment in this moment, right now.

Death and Life

- We've all encountered death in some form, but few of us have actively thought about our own deaths. You might even think the idea sounds morbid. If you do, you're in good company. Most of us spend a lot of energy to avoid thinking about death.

- When death comes close, we have a variety of means at our disposal to prevent it from disturbing us too much. Our minds often function in strange ways to help keep us from thinking much about death.

- These clever psychological dynamics dovetail with the way society itself treats death. Our primary approach as a culture is to stave it off for as long as possible. We try to mask any signs of the aging process that might suggest to ourselves and others that we are inching closer to our inevitable end.

- As the inevitability of death draws nearer, we attempt to keep death at bay by prolonging life artificially with advanced medical technology, often choosing to ignore the diminished quality of life such technology brings.

- When at last death arrives, we often experience it as a defeat rather than as a natural stage of living. Then, to further estrange us from the reality of death, we turn over the dead to a commercial funeral home, which takes care of every aspect of disposing of the body so we don't have to.

- Long gone are the days when families brought the dead into their own homes where they themselves cared for the remains of their loved ones and came to terms with death in their individual ways.

- Removing death from of our midst and disguising its approach has further contributed to our fear of this reality, thus mystifying death and leaving us unprepared for it. What's more, our inordinate fear of death has taken away one of our greatest teachers for living life.

Reflecting on Death

- Contrary to the prevailing attitudes of the modern Western culture, the mindfulness tradition suggests that reflecting on death is not only liberating, but it's essential to living a full, satisfying life.

- Buddhism is by no means the only tradition to encourage the practice of contemplating death. Meditation on death and dying has a long history in the world's wisdom traditions.

- Reflecting on death, especially our own, makes us so familiar with it that we no longer fear it. In addition, when we no longer fear death, we can live more freely. To remove this terror helps bring us equanimity, which allows us to see the world and ourselves more clearly and to accept the fact of impermanence more completely.

- By fully accepting the inevitability of death with a calm mind, we come to greater clarity about what is really important in life. In the light of death, trivialities begin fall away.

- Because we forget that our lives are transitory, we are prone to conflict over matters that are of little consequence. When we hold before our minds the inevitability of our death, we recognize that such inconsequential things are not worth the fight.

- As we've noted many times, intellectually agreeing with the idea of impermanence is not sufficient. To take away the fear of death and enable us to live our life joyously in the face of it, we need specific practices that help us to embrace this wisdom on a deep and unqualified level.

Death Awareness Meditation

- There are a variety of different forms of mindfulness exercises that will allow you to bring awareness to the fact of your own finitude and clear the way for the insights that awareness provides.

- You may not find each of the following exercises equally valuable. Some you might find too frightening to practice at this stage of your journey. You are certainly free to choose which exercises are most meaningful to you.

- We've all been conditioned to live within a culture that is terribly fearful of death, so please extend compassion to yourself and engage those offerings that you feel you can reasonably handle.

- Perhaps the easiest and least intimidating form of meditating on death is the Buddhist practice of reciting the Five Remembrances. These recitations are straightforward observations about life's fragility, and simply contemplating them can help open us to the deeper acceptance of our impermanence and the great benefits that acceptance confers.

- If you wish, you may recite each of the following statements.

  o I am subject to aging. Aging is unavoidable.

  o I am subject to illness. Illness is unavoidable.

o I am subject to death. Death is unavoidable.

o I will be separated and parted from everyone and everything that is dear to me.

o Whatever I do, for good or for ill, that will I reap.

- Another series of statements known as the Nine Meditations on Death makes many of the same points as the Five Remembrances but puts them in different language and elaborates some of their insights.

- If you wish, you may recite each of the following statements.

    o There is no possible way to escape death. No one ever has, not even Jesus or the Buddha.

    o Life has a definite limit, and each moment brings us closer to our death.

    o We are dying from the moment we are born.

    o Death comes in a moment, and its time is uncertain. All that separates us from death is one breath.

    o The duration of our lifespan is uncertain. The young can die before the old, and the healthy can die before the sick.

    o There are many causes and circumstances that lead to death.

    o The weakness and fragility of one's physical body contribute to life's uncertainty. The body can be easily destroyed by disease or accident.

- o Worldly possessions such as wealth, position, and money cannot help us with the reality of death. Our relatives and friends cannot help us.

- o Even our own precious body is of no help. We will leave it behind like an empty shell.

- Like the Five Remembrances, the Nine Meditations can be memorized or written down and recited each day. You're free to vary the language to make these reflections more personally meaningful.

- While our culture encourages us to avoid death, traditional Asian societies tend to keep the face of death in open view. In India, for example, the most common funeral is an open-air cremation preceded by a procession through the town or village where the body of the deceased is easily visible.

- Buddhist monastics and Hindu holy men and women would take this exposure to death even further by going to the funeral grounds to practice meditation. The practice was intended, of course, to teach these ascetics to become familiar with death and thus help eliminate their fear of it.

- In some countries in South and Southeast Asia, Buddhist monks were directed to go to secluded fields where corpses had been left in the open rather than buried or burned. There, they would go each day to observe the body in a gradual state of decomposition. They were encouraged to think of the decaying corpses as their own.

- If you're inclined, you might try a variation of this exercise. Go to a graveyard, find a spot to sit, and begin breathing meditation. When your mind is clear and focused, deliberately think about the graves around you. Imagine yourself in such a grave. Imagine your body slowly combining with the soil.

- Take your time with this practice, and try to think of every aspect you can of the physical and chemical changes that will occur to your body after your death. If you feel fear or other emotions arising while you do this, be sure to pay attention. Feel your emotions as completely as you can, and then let them go. Notice and appreciate the way that the idea of your own death affects you.

A Guided Meditation for Death Awareness

- The final example of death awareness meditation is a guided reflection in which you are invited to participate by imagining the described experiences. You can practice this meditation sitting or lying down in *shavasana*, the corpse pose we used in the body scan meditation.

- When you're prepared, sit or lie down on your back in a supine position. Take a few deep breaths, and become attentive to the inhalation and exhalation as the breath returns to its natural rhythm. Focus your attention for a few moments on the sensation of breathing.

- As you breathe, imagine a large box beside you. Picture the box as empty. Now, think of your loved ones, your family and friends, one at a time. Hear each person's voice; think of them laughing and seeing them smile. Imagine embracing each one of them. Summon the love you feel for each person.

- Now, put each person in the box beside you. Imagine that he or she disappears upon stepping into the box. There is room for every friend and every family member—and yet the box is empty. Notice that you are alone. Reflect on how you feel when you realize that your friends and family are all gone.

- Now, picture all the rooms where you live. In your mind, look at what's on the walls and on the tables. See your bed, your books, and your other possessions. Put all the furniture in the box. Now, put all your favorite clothes and jewelry in the box. Watch the box become empty.

- Imagine that you are in your house. Take the walls, the doors, and the windows—the entire house itself—and put them in the box. If you have a car, put it in the box. See the box become empty.

- Notice everything in your neighborhood. Imagine the sounds you hear when you step outside. Imagine how it feels to have the air on your face as you move. Take a good look at everything you see, and put it in the box. See the box become empty.

- Now, search for memories of places you have been and people you have known. As you think of them, cherish them, and then put them in the box. Put everything in the box—memories, music, trees, grass, and even the sky. All that is left is you and the box.

- See the box become empty. Now, put yourself in the box. See the box become empty. See the box disappear. See only emptiness. Be with this moment. Notice what you feel. Feel it fully. Death will come in an ordinary moment just like this one.

- Now, return your awareness to the breath. Feel your heart beating. Notice how wonderful it is to be alive.

- When you are ready to end the meditation, slowly move your fingers and toes and then your arms and legs. Feel the floor beneath you. Open your eyes and gently stretch. Notice how your body feels. Give yourself ample time before you get up.

- Now is a good time to remember the importance of treating yourself with compassion, and be compassionate with yourself if you found this meditation hard to practice. Take a few moments to be grateful for where you are and who you are—right now.

1. What was your first experience with death? When did you come to know that you will one day die? How have those experiences affected your outlook on death today?

2. Assess how comfortable you are with your own impermanence.

Life—Putting It All in Perspective
Lecture 24

The Buddha always encouraged his followers to take a critical eye toward anyone claiming to present the truth and to judge the veracity of any claim or practice for themselves. In a famous statement, he urges them never to accept anything as true simply because it is said to be revelation, because it is traditional, because it comes from sacred texts, or because the teacher seems competent. Rather, he said, when you know for yourself that something is wholesome, blameless, and leads to benefit and happiness, then you should accept it and abide in it.

Putting Mindfulness in Perspective

- In this course, we have looked at the fundamental components of the practice of mindfulness and have discussed a great many areas of life in which these practices can be beneficially exercised.

- If there is anything about that practice that remains unclear, return to the lectures and read them again. Reading the lectures again— and still again—may prove valuable.

- It might be helpful to find a couple of books on basic mindfulness practice and read those as well. You'll readily see that different meditation teachers teach the discipline in slightly—and sometimes substantially—different ways.

- You may find that what other teachers have to say about mindfulness practice is more meaningful to you than what has been taught in this course. The practice is simple but extremely rich.

- A word of caution: Beware of spending too much time with the lectures or reading too many books about meditation. These activities can easily become ends in themselves—to the point that you're studying the practice of meditation rather than practicing the practice of meditation.

- Once you've understood the essential features of the discipline and have become comfortable doing them, begin to trust yourself to customize the practice to suit your own individual qualities.

- In this series, we've discussed and demonstrated a wide range of exercises. Not all of them, certainly, were equally appealing. Take as much as you can from each of them. Some you'll want to practice just as explained, others you may want to vary a bit, and still others may have no appeal at all.

- However, resist dismissing any exercise immediately. If a practice carries little meaning for you now, revisit it later. The practices we dislike the most are often the ones from which we gain the greatest benefit.

- If you have the opportunity to study with a reputable teacher of mindfulness meditation, try to take to take advantage of it. A good teacher can answer questions or concerns you may have in ways that are not possible with a series of lectures.

- The trick is to ensure that a potential teacher is a good one, which is not always an easy thing to do. As you may know, there are many teachers, sages, preachers, evangelists, missionaries, and gurus out there who are eager to tell you what to believe and how to live your life.

Following Up with Mindfulness

- As you proceed with your daily practice, you may consider at some point to intensify your meditation experience with a retreat. There are many types of retreats, and each can be very beneficial for your practice. Perhaps the simplest is to dedicate a day to mindfulness in the comfort of your own home.

- Try to arrange to be alone and quiet for four to eight hours—more if you're able—where you do nothing other than practice. You can design this self-retreat in any way that suits you, but it ought to include alternating sitting and walking practice.

- If you choose, you can add a body scan, mindful eating, and listening to a recorded talk on mindfulness. There are many locations on the Internet where you can download such talks.

- If you search the Internet, you'll also find plenty of listings for other kinds of retreats. There are a growing number of retreat centers across the country and throughout the world that offer retreats lasting from a weekend to three months to the traditional three-year, three-month, three-day retreat taken by some very committed practitioners.

- A very popular type of retreat in the mindfulness tradition lasts for ten days. In a ten-day retreat, you're usually with other practitioners, sitting and walking for as much as 16 hours a day—all in silence. A retreat of this length will benefit your practice (and the rest of your life) enormously.

- The most important thing about practicing mindfulness is: Just do it. It's difficult to get started sometimes, and it's difficult to continue, but the rewards are immeasurable.

Mindfulness and Life

- Meditation, of course, does more than just provide a quiet refuge. It also profoundly alters the way you view yourself, the world, and your place in it.

- When you study a lot of traditions, it is hard not to take away something from each one that impacts the way you live and view the world. Even for a viewpoint or practice that you would never dream of adopting wholesale, you should always find something worth affirming.

- In addition, views sometimes change, and you should always remain open to that change. Being firmly attached to beliefs and perspectives, as mindfulness practice suggests, can lead to great confusion and quarreling.

- The Buddha even cautioned his students not to become attached to his teachings. He told his students that his teachings are a raft. When you use a raft to get from one side of the lake to the other, you don't pick it up and carry it around with you. You leave it on the shore.

- Subverting the notion of a fixed identity is one of the things a mindfulness practice will do for you. And best of all, it can help you be comfortable without having a fixed identity.

- Gaining insight into the transience of the self enables you to think of yourself as a fluid reality, unable to be adequately named by conventional labels.

- Underneath the words you might use to identify yourself lies a reality that is a genuine mystery—at once conscious and self-aware, interrelated with the rest of the cosmos, and yet unfathomable in its depth.

- Likewise, the practice of mindfulness can alter your understanding of ultimate reality—the underlying nature of the universe and the ultimate power that governs the universe—to allow you to feel at home with its mystery.

- Mindfulness can encourage you to feel immense awe and happiness at being able to marvel at this world and our lives in it without having to provide a comprehensive and systematic explanation for the entire universe.

Lessons from Mindfulness

- Within the joyous mystery that surrounds and permeates our lives, mindfulness practice allows us to affirm some very simple things about living that has struck many individuals as being true.

- One simple realization is the acknowledgement that our control over life, like our knowledge of it, is very limited indeed. Mindfulness permits us to see clearly how little control we really have over the events that profoundly affect us.

- Much of our suffering, we realize, is caused by our dogged efforts to try to command these things over which we have no authority, but the practice also allows us to recognize that we have a capacity to shape our minds in ways that are wholesome for us and for others.

- With the training that mindfulness practice provides, we can learn to develop our minds in ways that allow us to relinquish the need to control and to accept reality as it is in this very moment.

One of the central insights of mindfulness practice is seeing the interrelatedness of reality.

- Mindfulness practice also teaches us that everything we do, think, and say has an important effect—particularly on our own character, but also in the lives others. With that recognition comes a responsibility to tend to our minds with great care.

- All we do and think shapes the quality of our character, and for that reason, it vitally important to be attentive to what we put in our minds and allow them to dwell on.

Mindfulness and Compassion

- Our species is at a critical juncture in its evolution. Perhaps because of our fragility, we always seem to be at a critical juncture.

- Today, we face a great number of global crises: addressing the great inequities between rich and poor, providing adequate food and health care to all people, dealing with serious environmental issues, coping with acts of terrorism, and coming to terms with a religious pluralistic world in which misunderstandings often lead to hatred.

- If there was ever a time that we needed to practice compassion, it's now. The problem is that many of us are not yet convinced of its importance, or if we are, we are insufficiently trained in how to practice it.

- The mindfulness discipline offers one very compelling way for us to grasp the importance of compassion and to learn how to implement it in our everyday life.

- A growing number of people around the world are beginning to see the necessity for us to devote more deliberate attention to the study and practice of compassion as a way to help address these massive issues that face us.

- Exercising compassion and kindness is one practice that the core of every religious tradition affirms. Religions may not be able to agree about the nature and existence of God, or they may have differing views of the soul and the ultimate destiny of human life. Religions certainly profess different doctrines and perform different rituals and ceremonies, but about the importance of being kind to others and oneself they seem to be in accord.

- One of the central insights of mindfulness practice is seeing the interrelatedness of reality. Once you see how your life is closely connected with that of others, you recognize that it is only with their support that you are able do anything at all.

- May each and every person—and, indeed, may all beings—be well and happy.

Questions to Consider

1. Which mindfulness exercises discussed in the series seem to have the most and the least appeal to you? Why?

2. What are the advantages and disadvantages of resisting fixed labels to define your identity?

Glossary

anger: The feeling of displeasure, usually accompanied by antagonism; it encompasses a wide range of experiences from simple irritation and annoyance to rage and fury.

attachment: The way in which people cling to the various items of their experiences as if they can't live without them.

bhavana: Most accurately translated as "cultivation," this is what Buddhism calls meditation. It does not mean deep thinking but, rather, the awareness and discipline that allow one to shape the mind in ways conducive to happiness and well-being.

Burmese style: In this position, one sits on a cushion, crossing the legs at the ankles without having to place the feet on opposite thighs—as when sitting on the floor.

compassion: The desire to alleviate suffering.

conditioning: The process of habitual thinking that significantly determines what people think, feel, and perceive. The more people entertain a particular thought or a particular kind of thought, the more their minds are prone to generate thoughts of that nature.

courage: The ability to accept suffering rather than flee from it; the determination to look at difficulty straight in the eye.

dana: The Buddhist word for generosity.

dukkha: A Buddhist term that basically means "suffering" and that denotes the fundamental frustrating, insatiable quality of the mindless existence of human beings.

Eightfold Path: In Buddhism, mindfulness is a component of this path, which leads to enlightenment and freedom from the cycle of continual rebirth.

ekgrata: The term that Hindu yogis use for concentration, or one-pointedness.

gatha: A short verse from the Buddhist tradition that focuses the mind on a wholesome thought.

generosity: The willingness to give to others; on a deeper level, it is the eagerness to relinquish anything that one might feel is a possession.

greed: The self-centered desire for unnecessary things; it is considered to be a poison of the mind because it distorts one's view of reality and leaves one unhappy.

grieving: The process of coming to terms with loss in life.

harsh speech: Speech that may be hurtful without any real intent to be so; the use of language that shows little or no regard for the feelings of others. It is usually thoughtless and includes profanity, sarcasm, and shouting.

idle chatter: Generic, inessential language whose basic purpose is to fill airspace; it is the verbal equivalent of unnecessary material possessions.

karma: The belief of many Hindus, Buddhists, and Jains that thoughts, deeds, and words from people's previous lives profoundly influence the mental states they have at birth.

labyrinth: Intricate structures or patterns that define a pathway; it has twists and turns but only a single route.

lotus position: In this traditional pose, one sits on the bare floor or a thin cushion and places the right foot on top of the left thigh and the left foot on top of the right thigh.

malicious speech: The Buddhist term for the practice of making hurtful assertions under the veil of truth. A malicious statement may be either true or false, but its objective is to harm.

mantra: A short saying or set of syllables that a meditator repeats to him- or herself.

maze: A kind of puzzle with many pathway options; one can get lost in a maze, and the goal is to find a way out.

meditation: Refers to certain exercises that can be used to enlarge and refine mindfulness. Not all forms of meditation, however, intend to cultivate mindfulness.

metta meditation: An ancient practice that has long been the cornerstone for cultivating compassion in the Buddhist tradition. "Metta" is a Buddhist term that usually translates as "loving-kindness."

mindfulness: The process of attentively observing an experience as it unfolds in a moment-by-moment awareness; it is devoid of the constant comparing and assessing that ordinarily occupies our mental functioning.

mindlessness: A mental state in which the mind generates a constant swirl of remarks and judgments that create a barrier of words and images that separate people from their lives. This condition makes it difficult to be mindful—or attentive—to life's experiences.

nirvana: A state of bliss; in Buddhism, it transcends suffering and karma.

not-knowing: A beginning practice that starts with an honest assessment of what one really knows and what one really can know.

not-self: A term that is sometimes compared to "insubstantiality." This is the third mark of existence that is central to the Buddhist worldview—and the most difficult to grasp both by intellect and by insight, even for those within the tradition.

pity: Feeling sorry for someone who has to endure suffering.

pleasure principle: A term introduced by Sigmund Freud that describes the way in which people grasp for the things they enjoy and evade the things they don't.

sati: A special form of heightened awareness that promotes the end of suffering and fosteres happiness and well-being for all; it is the Buddha's word that is translated into English as "mindfulness."

seiza: A posture that involves sitting on one's calves with the knees, shins, and feet resting on the ground. This manner of sitting is very common throughout Japan, even among those who do not practice meditation.

serendipity: The word for the phenomenon of discovering pleasant things not sought for. Part of the surprising and unpredictable quality of existence is the way that, sometimes, things can turn out better than imagined.

shavasana: This position is known as the corpse pose and is practiced in hatha yoga.

Upanishad: One of the earliest Hindu documents in which instructions in contemplative practice were recorded.

vipassana: The Buddhist word for "insights" or "clear gazing," these are unmistakable moments when a person sees things differently.

Bibliography

Armstrong, Karen. *Twelve Steps to a Compassionate Life*. New York: Alfred A. Knopf, 2011. Karen Armstrong is a popular religious writer who has called for greater attention to the study and practice of compassion. This work, strongly influenced by the mindfulness traditions, provides her outline for the development of compassion.

Bacovcin, Helen. *The Way of a Pilgrim and the Pilgrim Continues His Way: Spiritual Classics from Russia*. Garden City, NY: Image Books, 1978. I love this book. It's a memoir of a Russian peasant who learns the Jesus Prayer—part of the mindfulness tradition in Eastern Orthodoxy—and puts it into practice as he wanders through 19th-century Russia.

Batchelor, Stephen. *Buddhism without Beliefs: a Contemporary Guide to Awakening*. New York: Riverhead Books, 1998. A former Tibetan and Zen monk, Batchelor presents an understanding of Buddhism that attempts to make the tradition more accessible to modern sensibilities. Recommended.

Beck, Charlotte Joko, and Steve Smith. *Everyday Zen: Love and Work*. New York, NY: HarperOne, 2007. Charlotte Beck was a Zen teacher in San Diego. This is a surprising and lucid collection of her essays on a variety of subjects. Recommended.

Berger, K. T. *Zen Driving*. New York: Ballantine, 1988. Tips on how to incorporate mindfulness practice into your experience of driving.

Bernhard, Toni. *How to Be Sick: A Buddhist-Inspired Guide for the Chronically Ill and Their Caregivers*. Boston: Wisdom Publications, 2010. This moving book is a memoir of one woman's coming to terms with chronic illness and pain using the techniques of mindfulness practice. Recommended.

Bodhi, Bhikkhu. *The Noble Eightfold Path: Way to the End of Suffering*. Seattle, WA: BPS Pariyatti Editions, 2000. One of the clearest short presentations of the Buddha's path to awakening. Scholarly, yet very accessible to the lay audience.

Boyce, Barry Campbell. *The Mindfulness Revolution: Leading Psychologists, Scientists, Artists, and Meditation Teachers on the Power of Mindfulness in Daily Life.* Boston: Shambhala, 2011. This anthology is an excellent introduction to the concept and practice of mindfulness and the way it informs and transforms every aspect of life. Recommended.

Carroll, Michael. *Awake at Work: Facing the Challenges of Life on the Job.* Boston: Shambhala Publications, 2004. Practical advice for incorporating mindfulness practice in the work environment. Helpful for people with jobs!

Chah, Achaan. *Food for the Heart: The Collected Teachings of Ajahn Chah.* Boston: Wisdom Publications, 2002. An insightful collection of essays by a Thai Buddhist monk who was a teacher to many American meditators in the latter part of the 20th century.

Chödrön, Pema. *Start Where You Are: A Guide to Compassionate Living.* Boston: Shambhala, 2004. Pema Chödrön is a nun in the Shambhala Buddhist tradition and one of the most popular writers on mindfulness practices today. Any of her works are worth reading. This one on developing compassion is a good place to start.

Dermond, Susan Usha. *Calm and Compassionate Children: A Handbook.* Berkeley: Celestial Arts, 2007. One of the best resources for introducing mindfulness practices to children. Recommended.

Feldman, Christina. *Compassion: Listening to the Cries of the World.* Berkeley: Rodmell Press, 2005. A thorough and accessible study of the idea and practice of compassion. Contains useful exercises for developing this virtue.

Fetzer Institute Website. Accessed August 18, 2011. http://www.fetzer. org. This website is devoted to encouraging the practice of forgiveness and compassion.

Germer, Christopher K. *The Mindful Path to Self-Compassion: Freeing Yourself from Destructive Thoughts and Emotions*. New York: Guilford Press, 2009. A comprehensive analysis and practical guidebook for learning to extend compassion to one's self.

Goenka, S. N. Vipassana Meditation Website. Accessed August 18, 2011. http://www.dhamma.org/. Website for the organization that teaches mindfulness practices in the tradition of S. N. Goenka.

Goldstein, Joseph. *The Experience of Insight: A Simple and Direct Guide to Buddhist Meditation*. Boston: Shambhala Publications, 1987. As the subtitle rightly indicates, this guide to mindfulness meditation is both simple and direct.

Gunaratana, Henepola. *Beyond Mindfulness in Plain English: An Introductory Guide to Deeper States of Meditation*. Boston: Wisdom Publications, 2009. This guide is for those who have gained experience in the basic practices of mindfulness and are interested in taking the practice to the next level.

————. *Eight Mindful Steps to Happiness: Walking the Path of the Buddha*. Boston: Wisdom Publications, 2001. A comprehensive and understandable account of the Buddha's path to awakening. Helps to explain the relationships among the many components of the path.

————. *Mindfulness in Plain English*. Boston: Wisdom Publications, 2002. In my opinion, this book is by far the best written guide on how to practice mindfulness meditation. Highly recommended.

Hanson, Rick, and Richard Mendius. *Buddha's Brain: The Practical Neuroscience of Happiness, Love & Wisdom*. Oakland, CA: New Harbinger Publications, 2009. An accessible overview of the neuroscience of mindfulness practice.

Hart, William. *The Art of Living: Vipassana Meditation as Taught by S. N. Goenka*. San Francisco: Harper & Row, 1987. S. N. Goekna is a highly regarded Indian teacher of *vipassana* (insight) meditation. He learned his practice in Burma and has taught it throughout the world. This book explains his approach.

Kabat-Zinn, Jon. *Full Catastrophe Living: Using the Wisdom of Your Body and Mind to Face Stress, Pain, and Illness*. New York, NY: Delacorte Press, 1990. Jon Kabat-Zinn is a popular American physician, writer, and meditation instructor. This is one of his best books. It focuses on his specialty: using mindfulness to ease physical pain and suffering.

Kaza, Stephanie. *Hooked!: Buddhist Writings on Greed, Desire, and the Urge to Consume*. Boston: Shambhala, 2005. An informative anthology containing essays written from a variety of Buddhist perspectives on consumerism and greed in the modern world. Recommended.

Khema, Ayya. *Who Is My Self?: A Guide to Buddhist Meditation*. Boston: Wisdom Publications, 1997. Ayya Khema was a German who ordained as a Buddhist nun in the 20th century. Her writings on meditation and mindfulness practices are very lucid.

Kornfield, Jack. *A Path with Heart: A Guide through the Perils and Promises of Spiritual Life*. New York, NY: Bantam Books, 1993. Jack Kornfield is a highly respected American meditation teacher and an engaging storyteller. This is a good book for getting acquainted with mindfulness practices. Recommended.

Leloup, Jean-Yves, and M. S. Laird. *Being Still: Reflections on an Ancient Mystical Tradition*. Leominster, Herefordshire, UK: Gracewing, 2003. A fascinating book on mindfulness practice in the Eastern Orthodox tradition of Christianity.

McDonald, Michele. *Awake at the Wheel: Mindful Driving*. CD. More Than Sound Productions, 2011. This is an excellent audio CD for driving practice. I'm indebted to McDonald for her insights on mindful driving.

Mindful Website. Accessed August 18, 2011. http://mindful.org. Accessible website devoted to the practice of mindfulness in a wide range of areas.

Muesse, Mark W. "Cultivating a Quiet Mind." Explorefaith.org . Accessed August 18, 2011. http://www.explorefaith.org/prayer/meditation/questions_ and_answers_about_meditation.php?ht=. This is one of my own articles about the basics of meditation practice and its relationship to other contemplative practices in the world's religions.

Nhat Hạnh, Thich. *Guide to Walking Meditation.* Parallax Press, 2005. One of the few books dedicated solely to the practice of walking meditation. Like all of Thich Nhat Hanh's works, this book is highly accessible and easy to understand.

———. *Peace Is Every Step: The Path of Mindfulness in Everyday Life.* Shambhala Pubns, 2009. Another highly readable book by Thich Nhat Hanh.

Nhat Hạnh, Thich, and Mai Vo-Dinh. *The Miracle of Mindfulness: A Manual on Meditation.* Boston: Beacon Press, 1987. Probably the most accessible introduction to the concept and practice of mindfulness meditation. Recommended.

Phra, Thēpwisutthimēthī, and Santikaro Bhikkhu. *Mindfulness with Breathing: A Manual for Serious Beginners.* Boston: Wisdom Publications, 1997. Buddhadasa Bhikkhu (Phra Thēpwisutthimēthī) was a highly regarded Thai Buddhist monk. This text is a very clearly written and well-translated meditation manual. Recommended.

Rosenberg, Larry, and David Guy. *Breath by Breath: The Liberating Practice of Insight Liberation.* Boston: Shambhala, 1998. Rosenberg's clear explanation of the *Anapanasati Sutta,* one of the classic ancient texts on meditating on the breath. Recommended.

———. *Living in the Light of Death: On the Art of Being Truly Alive.* Boston: Shambhala, 2001. Larry Rosenberg is an excellent meditation teacher. This book focuses on his engagement with death awareness practices.

Salzberg, Sharon. *Loving-kindness: The Revolutionary Art of Happiness*. Boston: Shambhala, 1995. An easy-to-read guide to the basic loving-kindness meditation for the development of compassion.

Shaw, Sarah. *Introduction to Buddhist Meditation*. London: Routledge, 2009. More of a scholarly study of meditation in the Buddhist tradition focused on the ancient texts and manuals.

Siegel, Daniel J. *Mindsight: The New Science of Personal Transformation*. New York: Bantam Books, 2010. An integrative study of neuroscientific research on mindfulness and its application in psychotherapy.

Sīlānanda, U, and Ruth-Inge Heinze. *The Four Foundations of Mindfulness*. Boston: Wisdom Publications, 2002. The scripture on the four foundations of mindfulness are believed to represent the Buddha's basic teaching on meditation. This book by a Burmese monk is an effort to explain those teachings for a modern audience. The writing style can be difficult at times.

Snyder, Stephen, and Tina Rasmussen. *Practicing the Jhānas: Traditional Concentration Meditation as Presented by the Venerable Pa Auk Sayadaw*. Boston: Shambhala, 2009. This work is for those who are ready to begin more advanced mindfulness practices.

Sogyal, Patrick Gaffney, and Andrew Harvey. *The Tibetan Book of Living and Dying*. San Francisco, CA: HarperSanFrancisco, 2002. This work has become a modern classic on the Tibetan Buddhist understanding of mindful living. Recommended.

Somov, Pavel G. *Eating the Moment: 141 Mindful Practices to Overcome Overeating One Meal at a Time*. Oakland, CA: New Harbinger Publications, 2008. Very practical guide for learning to eat mindfully. Highly recommended.

Sumedho, Ajahn. *The Mind and the Way: Buddhist Reflections on Life*. Boston: Wisdom Publications, 1995. Ajahn Sumedho is one of my favorite Buddhist writers. This is a clear and highly insightful collection of his essays. Recommended.

————. *The Sound of Silence: The Selected Teachings of Ajahn Sumedho*. Boston: Wisdom Publications, 2007. Another excellent collection of Sumedho's essays.

Suzuki, Shunryu. *Zen Mind, Beginner's Mind*. Shambhala Pubns, 2011. A classic modern Zen text. Highly recommended.

Thera, Nyanaponika. *Satipatthāna: The Heart of Buddhist Meditation*. San Francisco, CA: Weiser Books, 2007. Well-informed and erudite explanation of mindfulness meditation based on the earliest Buddhist texts. Recommended for those with an academic interest in the practice.

Thubten, Chodron. *Working with Anger*. Ithaca, NY: Snow Lion Publication, 2001. A good work for learning how to cope with anger.

Tonkinson, Carole. *Wake Up and Cook: Kitchen Buddhism in Words and Recipes*. New York: Riverhead Books, 1997. This is both an anthology on mindful eating and a cookbook. Recommended.

Wallis, Glenn. *The* Dhammapada*: Verses on the Way*. New York: Modern Library, 2004. The *Dhammapada* is a classic wisdom text of Buddhism. It is written in an accessible, aphoristic form. Wallis's translation is one of the best. Highly recommended.

Walpola, Rāhula. *What the Buddha Taught*. New York: Grove Press, 1987. A classic in the field, this book remains one of the best introductions to the basic teachings of the Buddha over 50 years after its publication. Highly recommended.

Young, Shinzen. The Science of Meditation in Action. Accessed August 18, 2011. http://www.shinzen.org/. Website for Shinzen Young, a popular mindfulness teac

Notes

Notes

Notes

Notes